MW01469870

Road Map for the Baldrige Journey

Also available from ASQ Quality Press:

2015-2016 Baldrige Excellence Framework (Business/Nonprofit)
Baldrige Performance Excellence Program at NIST

2015-2016 Baldrige Excellence Framework (Health Care)
Baldrige Performance Excellence Program at NIST

2015-2016 Baldrige Excellence Framework (Education)
Baldrige Performance Excellence Program at NIST

Baldrige 20/20: An Executive's Guide to the Criteria for Performance Excellence
Baldrige Performance Excellence Program at NIST

Organization Diagnosis, Design, and Transformation, Seventh Edition: Baldrige Users Guide (BUG)
John Vinyard

Baldrige in Plain English: Understanding Performance Excellence
John Vinyard

Outcomes, Performance, Structure: Three Keys to Organizational Excellence
Michael E. Gallery and Stephen C. Carey

Journey to Excellence: How Baldrige Health Care Leaders Succeed
Kathleen J. Goonan, MD, Joseph A. Muzikowski, and Patricia K. Stoltz

Charting Your Course: Lessons Learned During the Journey Toward Performance Excellence
Robert Ewy and John G. Conyers

Transformation to Performance Excellence: Baldrige Education Leaders Speak Out
Sandra Cokeley, Margaret A. Byrnes, Geri Markley, and Suzanne Keely, editors

Root Cause Analysis: Simplified Tools and Techniques, Second Edition
Bjørn Andersen and Tom Fagerhaug

The Quality Toolbox, Second Edition
Nancy R. Tague

To request a complimentary catalog of ASQ Quality Press publications, call 800-248-1946, or visit our Web site at http://www.asq.org/quality-press.

Road Map for the Baldrige Journey

A Guide to Effective Use of the Criteria for Performance Excellence and Baldrige-based Award Programs

Joe Kilbride

ASQ Quality Press
Milwaukee, Wisconsin

American Society for Quality, Quality Press, Milwaukee, WI 53203
© 2015 by ASQ.
All rights reserved. Published 2015.
Printed in the United States of America.

20 19 18 17 16 15 5 4 3 2 1

Library of Congress Cataloging-in-Publication Data

Names: Kilbride, Joe, author.
Title: Road map for the Baldrige journey : a guide to effective use of the criteria for performance excellence and Baldrige-based award programs / by Joe Kilbride.
Description: Milwaukee, WI : ASQ Quality Press, 2015. | Includes bibliographical references and index.
Identifiers: LCCN 2015039491 | ISBN 9780873899208 (hardcover : alk. paper)
Subjects: LCSH: Malcolm Baldrige National Quality Award. | Total quality management. | Organizational effectiveness. | Performance.
Classification: LCC HD62.15 .K553 2015 | DDC 658.4/013—dc23
LC record available at http://lccn.loc.gov/2015039491

No part of this book may be reproduced in any form or by any means, electronic, mechanical, photocopying, recording, or otherwise, without the prior written permission of the publisher.

Publisher: Lynelle Korte
Acquisitions Editor: Matt T. Meinholz
Managing Editor: Paul Daniel O'Mara
Production Administrator: Randall Benson

ASQ Mission: The American Society for Quality advances individual, organizational, and community excellence worldwide through learning, quality improvement, and knowledge exchange.

Attention Bookstores, Wholesalers, Schools, and Corporations: ASQ Quality Press books, video, audio, and software are available at quantity discounts with bulk purchases for business, educational, or instructional use. For information, please contact ASQ Quality Press at 800-248-1946, or write to ASQ Quality Press, P.O. Box 3005, Milwaukee, WI 53201-3005.

To place orders or to request ASQ membership information, call 800-248-1946. Visit our Web site at www.asq.org/quality-press.

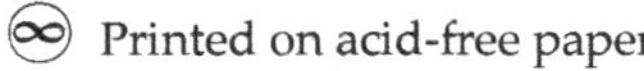

Quality Press
600 N. Plankinton Ave.
Milwaukee, WI 53203-2914
E-mail: authors@asq.org
The Global Voice of Quality®

Contents

List of Figures and Tables . . . . . . *vii*

Chapter 1 The Need for a Road Map **1**

Management is a Young Profession 1

How Will You Lead Your Organization Through the Coming Decade? 2

Baldrige Provides a Framework for Those in Pursuit of Excellence. 4

Criteria Describe the Destination but Do Not Provide Directions for the Journey. 4

A Detailed Road Map for the Journey 5

The Baldrige Framework 6

Overview of the Book. 7

Chapter 2 Scoring Guidelines Define Progress in the Journey to Excellence **11**

ADLI (Approach, Deployment, Learning, Integration). 11

Is This Just About Winning an Award? 15

BOM (Basic, Overall, Multiple) Allow You to Stage The Journey 20

Areas to Address Are the Building Blocks for Performance Excellence 24

Award Program a Source of Comprehensive, Objective Feedback 27

Chapter 3 Turn-by-turn Directions for the Journey.............. 29
Year One: Establish the Foundation, Structure, and Accountabilities........................... 31
Year Two and Beyond................................ 42
Summary of the Road Map 60

Chapter 4 Recommended Key Approaches for Categories 1–6.... 63
Leadership 64
Strategy.. 67
Customers 71
Measurement, Analysis, Knowledge Management... 74
Workforce... 79
Operations 83
Accelerating the Design of an Operating Model for Performance Excellence.................... 87

Chapter 5 Requirements for Category 7 Results 93
Category 7 Results are Usually an Afterthought 93
LeTCI Results Scoring Guidelines 94
Overall Requirements for Results.................. 101
Develop a Measurement System Aligned with Category 7 Results 107
Use Key Result Areas as a Planning and Measurement Framework to Ensure Alignment ... 111

Chapter 6 Integration of Planning and Measurement Systems with Key Results.................................. 115
Strategic Plan ties together elements from all Categories.................................. 115
Key Terms and Concepts.......................... 118
Guidance for Strategic Objectives.................. 127
Guidance for Strategic Measurement............... 131
Guidance for Goal Setting 142
Guidance for Action Plan Development 144
Guidance for Action Plan Deployment 150
The End... And Hopefully the Beginning of Your Journey 157
In Closing... 157

Notes *159*

Index *163*

List of Figures and Tables

Figure 1.1	Criteria overview: seven categories provide a comprehensive, integrated framework	6
Table 2.1	Process scoring guidelines	18
Table 2.2	Key differences in ADLI scoring dimensions	19
Figure 2.1	Explanation of Item format	21
Figure 3.1	CAP-Do process for systematic evaluation and improvement of key approaches	30
Table 3.1	Key factors in an Organizational Profile	32
Table 3.2	Key approach identification workshops	34
Table 3.3	Documentation of improvement history	41
Table 3.4	The annual cycle	43
Figure 3.2	Application process map in swim lane format	45
Table 3.5	Alignment of results OFIs with approaches in Categories 1–6	52
Table 4.1	Summary of key approaches recommended to meet overall requirements of Category 1	64
Table 4.2	Summary of key approaches recommended to meet overall requirements of Category 2	67
Table 4.3	Summary of key approaches recommended to meet overall requirements of Category 3	71
Table 4.4	Summary of key approaches recommended to meet overall requirements of Category 4	74
Table 4.5	Summary of key approaches recommended to meet overall requirements of Category 5	79
Table 4.6	Summary of key approaches recommended to meet overall requirements of Category 6	83
Table 4.7	A template to summarize senior leader communication methods	90
Table 4.8	Senior leadership communication process sample questions	91
Table 4.9	A template to document the history of improvements in senior leader communication methods	92

Table 5.1	LeTCI for evaluation of results	94
Table 5.2	Results scoring guidelines	95
Table 5.3	Key differences in results scoring at the basic and overall levels	97
Figure 5.1	Example of results format from Criteria response guidelines	100
Table 5.4	Overall requirements and LeTCI in multiple requirements for results items in Category 7	102
Figure 5.2	Key results areas required by Category 7 identify framework for planning and measurement	111
Figure 5.3	Education KRAs required by Category 7 identify framework for planning and measurement	112
Table 6.1	Example strategic plan summary	116
Figure 6.1	Item linkage in Categories 7, 2, 4	117
Table 6.2	Key terms and concepts for design of an integrated planning, measurement, and review system	119
Table 6.3	Examples of different ways to measure "speed of service"	132
Table 6.4	How you compete influences what you measure	138
Figure 6.2	Select comparisons, set goals	139
Table 6.5	Set goals based on the level of performance required	139
Figure 6.3	The value of projections and comparisons	142
Table 6.6	What/Who/When template for action plans	146
Table 6.7	Action plan template with the addition of in-process measures	149
Figure 6.4	Deployment requires translation of plans and goals at each level	152
Table 6.8	Planning and performance review calendar	155

1
The Need for a Road Map

MANAGEMENT IS A YOUNG PROFESSION

Have you ever been to Europe? During my first trip there one of my strongest impressions was the age of its most famous sites. Notre-Dame Cathedral in Paris was built in the twelfth century, more than 100 years before Columbus discovered America. The Tower of London was built in 1078. The Roman Colosseum dates to A.D. 70 and the Parthenon in Athens to the fifth century B.C. Though obvious in retrospect, my first experience of Europe made me acutely aware that by comparison, the United States is a very young nation.

I was struck by a similar observation about the profession of management while reading Walter Kiechel's 2012 *Harvard Business Review* article titled "The Management Century." Kiechel states that the management profession essentially came into being in the 1880s and in the century since has had a dramatic impact on the world in which we work.[1] It follows logically that management is a relatively young profession, that the work of leading organizations is in the early stages of development, and that management practices would benefit from clear direction and a means of continual refinement.

Management was to be viewed as a set of practices that could be studied and improved.

– Walter Kiechel III, *HBR* Nov. 2012[2]

Not only is management a young profession, it is also a very difficult one. My experience working with executives suggests that leading an organization of any size is a complex endeavor. It requires:

- Balancing the needs and expectations of a wide variety of stakeholders,
- Understanding the cause–effect relationship between multiple variables in the organization and its operating environment, and
- Determining optimal courses of action when faced with an uncertain future.

The relative immaturity of the profession combined with its challenging nature may help to explain the difficulties experienced by organizational leaders who are almost universally smart, hardworking, and well-intentioned. Their profession is in its early stages, and to some extent they are the ones defining its practice. It follows that these pioneers in the practice of organizational leadership would benefit from a road map that allows them to navigate the difficulties inherent in leading complex organizations and provides them with a method to refine their own practice for doing so.

To be clear, the intent here is not to provide an instruction manual for leading a complex organization. No such thing exists. Instead, the term *road map* is being used in two senses. One is consistent with its definition, as a detailed plan to guide progress toward a goal. In this case the goal is to become an excellent organization, one that is successful now and will remain so in the future.

The other use of the term is to suggest that the road map serves to guide those who are committed to leading their organization on a journey of some duration and difficulty. When the destination is excellence, we are not talking about a quick trip but rather about a learning journey that takes time and will invariably involve unexpected twists and turns along the way. In that sense, the road map provided here is intended to serve as a guide for those who are committed to leading their organizations on a journey of discovery, where organizational success and sustainability are the intended destination.

HOW WILL YOU LEAD YOUR ORGANIZATION THROUGH THE COMING DECADE?

The need for a road map is even greater when one is navigating unfamiliar or uncertain terrain. Think about your own organization and its operating environment. What will it look like in 2025? Leaders in every sector understand that the next ten years are likely to be extremely challenging. In the face of this uncertainty, many are seeking effective methods to lead their organizations through the decade ahead:

- Health care in the United States is in the midst of a dramatic change as reimbursement models shift from payment based on the volume of services delivered to improvement of health outcomes, reduction of costs, and effective population management.
- With the adoption of Common Core State Standards, education is facing a challenge similar in magnitude to the one encountered after passage of the No Child Left Behind Act in 2001.
- In the service sector, the internet and web-based technologies have significantly increased competition by making it possible to deliver many types of service from virtually anywhere in the world directly to your phone or mobile device.
- Manufacturing has undergone successive waves of change since the 1960s, with the most recent being the emergence of China as a dominant force. Some think 3D printing will be the next great disruptive innovation to upend the business models and supply chains of manufacturers globally.
- And changing demographics will have a significant impact on every sector in the coming years as the baby boomers retire and hand over responsibility for leadership to the next generation.

Organizations in every sector must be able to change and adapt if they are to thrive in the coming decade. How will your organization manage the changes ahead? Will you react to one challenge after another? Or will you adopt a proven assessment framework and use it as your platform for organizational transformation? The road map described here provides a well-defined approach that will enable leaders to identify and manage the changes needed to become and remain successful. It is based on a time-tested and validated set of requirements for becoming a world class organization, the Criteria for Performance Excellence. And it utilizes Baldrige-based state award programs as an inexpensive means to receive objective feedback and enable mid-course corrections as your operating environment and competitive situation changes.

The Baldrige Criteria is probably the single most influential document in the modern history of American business.

– Gordon Black, Former Chairman and CEO, Harris/Black International Ltd.[3]

BALDRIGE PROVIDES A FRAMEWORK FOR THOSE IN PURSUIT OF EXCELLENCE

In 1987 the Malcolm Baldrige National Quality Improvement Act was signed into law with the goal of improving the competitiveness of U.S. businesses. Soon thereafter, the Baldrige Award Program was created as a way to identify and recognize role-model organizations and share best practices, and the Criteria for Performance Excellence were established to evaluate award applicants.

The Criteria are revised every two years to ensure they continue to reflect validated, leading-edge practices for performance excellence. After 25 years of continuous improvement there is a compelling argument that they represent the most comprehensive and rigorous framework available for organizational assessment and improvement, not only in the United States but globally. In fact the Criteria are the model for approximately 100 performance excellence frameworks used by award programs around the world. Baldrige and other award programs are appealing for the recognition they bring to organizations, but many leaders have recognized that the value of the assessment and improvement process is much greater.

I see the Baldrige process as a powerful set of mechanisms for disciplined people engaged in disciplined thought and taking disciplined action to create great organizations that produce exceptional results.

– Jim Collins, author of *Good to Great: Why Some Companies Make the Leap…and Others Don't.*[4]

CRITERIA DESCRIBE THE DESTINATION BUT DO NOT PROVIDE DIRECTIONS FOR THE JOURNEY

While the Baldrige Criteria for Performance Excellence are one of the most widely known assessment frameworks in the world, interest in the Criteria has ebbed and flowed over the years. In part this may be due to the fact that applicants are often on their own when it comes to determining how to use the Criteria and award programs in an efficient and effective manner.

This difficulty is somewhat by design, since the Criteria for Performance Excellence are non-prescriptive.[5] The requirements are presented as more than 200 questions written in a generic manner to enable their application by all types of organizations. They do not tell leaders what to do to meet the requirements, which is both good and bad. While this allows organizations to develop processes to respond to the Criteria in ways that meet their unique needs, it has created a barrier for some leaders. This is particularly true in smaller organizations or those sectors that are less mature in the development of their management systems. Many leaders accept that the Criteria offer a proven and practical framework but are unclear how to use them most effectively. The typical answer given is to invest in training, serve as examiners, and begin the challenging learning process required to understand, translate, and apply the Criteria in their own organization. All this is helpful but does not provide a clear road map for effective use of the Criteria.

A DETAILED ROAD MAP FOR THE JOURNEY

This book adds to the typical answer and provides a detailed road map and systematic process to design and implement a customized operating model for performance excellence based on the Criteria. The road map includes regular use of state award programs for external feedback to enable mid-course correction. Though recognition is not its primary purpose, following this road map also increases the likelihood of being recognized by these award programs. The approach presented here will not guarantee an award, but it will help an organization's leaders use the Criteria and award programs more efficiently and effectively as an aid to organizational transformation and improvement.

This road map is the product of my work since 1995 as a consultant, examiner, judge, and trainer of new examiners for Illinois' state award program. It synthesizes the best practices learned from applicants, clients, and many others over the years. In fact, it was from working closely with effective leaders in successful organizations that I became aware of the need for a well-defined and structured approach.

Many leaders of successful organizations are seeking a way to move their organization from good to great in the near-term and to ensure the organization's sustainability for the long-term. Effective leaders often reach a point when they begin to reflect upon their legacy and become concerned that the organization's current success is too dependent on the insights and actions of its key leaders. They recognize that an organization capable of producing excellent results for the long-term must shift away from being person-dependent and instead weave the approaches that are producing their current results into the very fabric of the organization's processes and culture. It is not surprising that these leaders find the Criteria offer a valuable blueprint for building an integrated system for performance excellence. It is also not surprising that they become frustrated to find there is not a well-defined method for doing so. This book attempts to meet that need and provide a systematic process to guide organizational transformation. It is written specifically for those leaders who are committed to using the Criteria and their state award program to design and implement a Baldrige-based operating model that will enable their organization to achieve and sustain excellence.

THE BALDRIGE FRAMEWORK

For those who are relatively new to the Baldrige framework, Figure 1.1 provides an overview of the Criteria for Performance Excellence. The system consists of six process categories (1-6) that define the key approaches required to consistently deliver excellent results (7).

Categories 1, 2, and 3 are often referred to as the leadership triad. In simplest terms, senior leaders (Category 1) must set direction and establish clear performance expectations for the organization. Strategic plans are developed (Category 2) to define the strategies, goals, and plans needed to meet these expectations. To be effective these strategies must enable the organization to meet the needs of its customers (Category 3) better than others within the markets it serves.

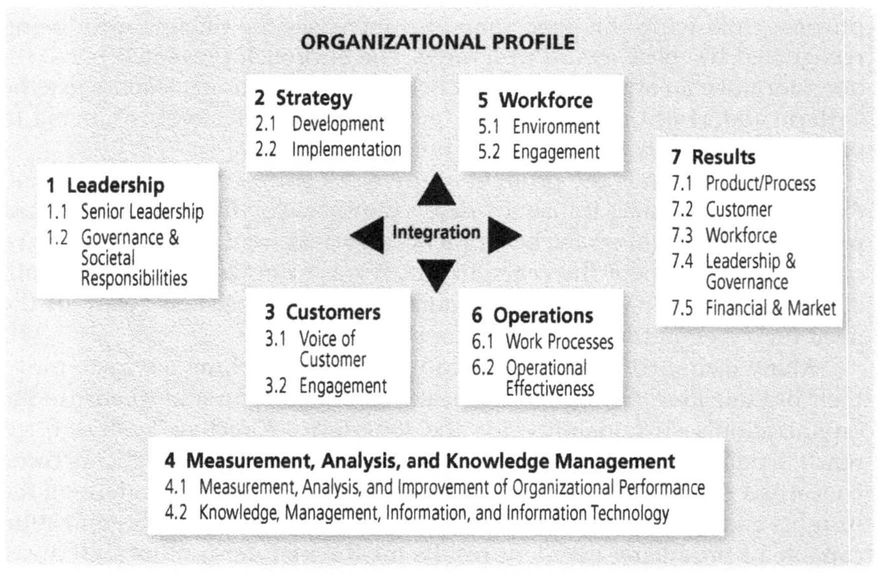

Figure 1.1 Criteria overview – seven categories provide a comprehensive, integrated framework.

Organizations in every sector implement strategy through the efforts of skilled and motivated staff (Category 5) who operate efficient and effective processes (Category 6). The systems foundation (Category 4) is used to report the performance results achieved (Category 7) and provide feedback to senior leaders (in Category 1) on the performance of the key processes (in Categories 2, 3, 5, and 6) that are producing those results.

The word *integration* at the center of the figure shows that all elements of the system are interrelated. The Organizational Profile at the top of the diagram sets the context for evaluation of an organization. The Criteria requirements in Categories 1–7 are intentionally generic so as to apply to any organization in any sector. The Organizational Profile allows the applicant to describe its unique operating environment so that examiners can determine the key factors to consider when evaluating its key processes and results.

The seven Categories have been summarized but the assessment process operates at the Item level. Note that Categories 1–6 each include two Items. For example, Category 1 Leadership consists of Item 1.1 Senior Leadership and Item 1.2 Governance and Societal Responsibilities. Applicants define their processes and results at the Item level. Examiners develop feedback comments and scores at the Item level. The 12 process and five results items provide a comprehensive, integrated framework for leaders to design their organization's Baldrige-based operating model for performance excellence. Other elements of the Baldrige Excellence Framework include the core values and concepts and the scoring guidelines. The latter are described in Chapter 2.

OVERVIEW OF THE BOOK

Design Your Organization's Operating Model for Excellence

Chapter 2 explains the rationale for the road map that is provided in subsequent chapters. This requires diving into the details of the Baldrige scoring guidelines that define the journey to organizational excellence. It introduces the ADLI (Approach, Deployment, Learning, and Integration) evaluation factors used by examiners to evaluate the processes presented by applicants in response to the requirements in Categories 1–6 of the Criteria. The approach dimension is further divided into basic, overall, and multiple (BOM) requirements. An understanding of ADLI, BOM, and the 28 areas to address within Categories 1–6 of the Criteria are the basis for the road map that will be used to stage an organization's journey over time. The recommended approach is to use the 28 areas to address and the overall requirements as the starting point to define and deploy the key approaches required by the Criteria. These key approaches become your organization's operating model for performance excellence.

Use a Baldrige-Based Award Program to Course Correct

Once the operating model is defined, the organization uses its state Baldrige-based award program as a source of external feedback to evaluate and improve its key approaches so that over time they evolve to meet the multiple requirements of most importance to your organization.

A system cannot understand itself. The transformation requires a view from the outside.

– W. Edwards Deming, *The New Economics for Industry, Government, and Education*.[6]

The external feedback you receive from award programs is often frustrating but can also be invaluable. The benefits of regular participation in an application and feedback process are the following:

- By applying every year you create an urgency and accountability for continual improvement.
- Preparing the workforce for site visits creates interest among employees that can be used to enhance their understanding and the deployment of key approaches.
- Site visits provide managers opportunities for reflection and learning during interviews with examiners. The "outside eyes" offered by examiners from various sectors can be a key factor in stimulating the organizational transformation required for the journey to excellence.
- Because the feedback you receive is Criteria-based, it requires the organization's leaders to develop a deeper understanding of the requirements and to think critically about how to improve and align the organization's key approaches in ways that respond most effectively to the key challenges of your unique operating environment.
- The opportunity for your leaders to participate as examiners allows them to develop expertise in the Criteria and to benchmark the approaches to excellence used by other organizations.
- The desire to improve with each successive application will cause the leadership team to prioritize its key approaches, key customers, key requirements, key goals, and key results. For most organizations the third application is very different from the first and this is primarily a result of senior leaders clarifying their focus and the organization's priorities over time.

- The awards received from a state program at each stage of the journey provide leaders the opportunity to recognize the workforce for their accomplishments and to build momentum for continual change.

Chapter 3 provides turn-by-turn directions for the journey to excellence. It is detailed and specific by design. Most readers who set out on their own journey will find this a useful starting point as they chart a course for their organization. The directions include identifying approximately 30 key approaches that correspond to the areas to address within Categories 1–6. The organization assigns an owner with responsibility to document each key approach. Key approach documentation is then used as the basis for award applications, as an aid to deploy the key approaches, and as the means to record the history of learning that results from scheduled, semi-annual cycles of evaluation and improvement of each key approach. They are also used by managers as an aid during site visits to provide the evidence required by examiners, and they enable you to make improvements based on opportunities identified in the feedback reports received at the conclusion of each award cycle.

Chapter 4 summarizes the key approaches that are recommended as an initial operating model to meet the overall requirements for 28 areas to address in Categories 1-6. Each organization's operating model will differ from this recommendation, but beginning with these key approaches can make the early stages of your journey more efficient. Without this guidance, organizations that do not understand the Criteria may take a number of wrong turns early in the process. Clients of Kilbride Consulting, Inc. are provided detailed templates to further accelerate the effort to design their organization's operating model.

Chapter 5 explains the requirements of Category 7 and recommends that you design some key approaches to ensure they are aligned with and produce the results required in Category 7. In the first few years of the journey, many organizations resist making the changes in their planning, measurement, and reporting systems that are required to meet the requirements for Category 7. Instead they try to force fit their current measurements to these requirements. For organizations that are committed long-term to the journey for excellence, it is recommended that they spend time early on to understand and adapt their approaches for planning and performance measurement in order meet the requirements for Category 7 results.

Chapter 6 provides guidance on how the planning processes in Category 2 and the measurement and review processes in Category 4 should be integrated and aligned to meet the requirements for results in Category 7. This builds on the discussion of results in Chapter 5 and provides guidance on possible alignment of key approaches that can help an organization:

- Meet the requirements for Category 7 results
- Focus the organization on achievement of its key goals and objectives
- Ensure an effective, fact-based system for review and improvement of performance

Before proceeding, it is recommended that you obtain a copy of the Baldrige Criteria for Performance Excellence for your sector. You can purchase the Criteria as PDF downloads on the Baldrige website or as printed booklets from ASQ.

Let your journey to organizational excellence begin.

2

Scoring Guidelines Define Progress in the Journey to Excellence

This chapter dives head first into the Baldrige scoring guidelines and the structure of the Criteria requirements. If you are not already familiar with these, you may find some of this confusing. It is necessary to provide the rationale for the road map used to stage an organization's journey to excellence over time. The recommended approach will be to use the overall requirements for the 28 areas to address in Categories 1–6 to define your organization's operating model, and then to use the feedback from your state award program to learn your way to excellence over time. The rest of this chapter explains what all that means and why this is the recommended approach.

ADLI (APPROACH, DEPLOYMENT, LEARNING, INTEGRATION)

An application for a Baldrige or state award includes two very different types of information. In responding to the questions in Categories 1–6, the applicant describes the *processes* used to meet Criteria requirements. In Category 7, the applicant reports *results* that summarize current performance levels and trends for areas such as product/service quality, customer satisfaction, workforce engagement, and financial and market results.

When examiners review an applicant's processes in Categories 1–6, they evaluate the maturity of the approaches that are described based on four factors: Approach, Deployment, Learning, and Integration. The ADLI evaluation factors are used by examiners to develop feedback comments and scores for each item. More importantly for our purposes, ADLI defines the steps in the journey to excellence. For each item in the Criteria organizations are required to:

- Establish an approach (A) that is systematic and effective
- Deploy (D) the approach to those units or groups where it makes sense

- Evaluate whether the approach is effective so you can learn (L) how to improve it
- Align the individual approaches to create an integrated (I) system that meets the organization's needs

ADLI and PDCA

Most readers will recognize that the *ADLI* dimensions of the Baldrige scoring guidelines are very similar to the PDCA (Plan, Do, Check, Act) cycle that is the most well-known approach to improvement.

- **Plan** is similar to *Approach*. Both suggest you begin by determining *how* you will do something. In the Criteria, approach refers to a process or a collection of methods that is used to meet an item requirement. Baldrige requires that each approach be systematic and effective. Systematic approaches are "well-ordered, repeatable, and use data and information so that learning is possible.[7]" In other words, processes should be defined and repeatable enough that you can evaluate and improve their effectiveness over time. This differs from some models, for which documentation and standardization are a primary focus. For Baldrige, the reason for systematic processes is to enable them to become more efficient and effective (i.e., mature) over time.
- **Do** is similar to *Deploy* and refers to application of the approach. Baldrige requires that you deploy each process as appropriate, i.e., where it makes sense. The scoring guidelines for deploy allow an organization to gradually expand the use of key approaches over time. Remember, it is a journey.
- **Check** and **Act** are similar to the evaluation and improvement that is required by the *Learning* dimension of the scoring guidelines. Baldrige not only requires that you do certain things but also that you continually get better at each of them over time. For example, it is not enough that you have a good process for strategic planning or complaint management or hiring. You are expected to improve each of these key processes over time.

The Learning dimension of the ADLI scoring guidelines suggests that an organization's approach to improvement should evolve from reactive problem solving to fact-based, systematic evaluation and improvement. In addition, the approaches used should improve both the efficiency and effectiveness of key processes and these improvements should be shared to enhance learning across the entire organization. Finally, the approaches for improvement should result in some innovation, i.e., something that is new or results in breakthrough improvement.

Integration is a Turning Point

The *Integration* dimension of ADLI goes beyond PDCA in several ways. When reviewing the integration (I) dimension of the scoring guidelines in Table 2.1, you find the terms *alignment* and *integration* at different scoring levels. In the 30-45% scoring band, alignment requires that individual approaches are not in conflict. As a simple example, if an organization's key goals focus on improvement of customer satisfaction but the approach used to evaluate individual employee performance is focused solely on the volume of customers they serve (and not the quality of service provided), it would suggest that these two processes are misaligned.

At higher levels, alignment requires that processes are designed and managed to meet an organization's key requirements. The aim is not only to get better at what you do but also to improve each process in ways that allow you to better meet organizational and customer requirements.

Integration goes beyond PDCA by requiring that individual processes be linked together to form a system. The Baldrige glossary definition of *integration* states that "Effective integration goes beyond alignment and is achieved when the individual components of a performance management system operate as a fully interconnected unit."

The integration (I) dimension is where the Baldrige framework often yields its greatest benefit. Once an organization has established its key approaches (A), deployed them (D), and begun to evaluate and improve them (L), it is typical to experience some improvement in results. However, the true benefit of the Baldrige framework comes from the multiplier effect that occurs when key approaches are:

- Designed and managed to meet key organizational needs (alignment) and
- Linked together to create a fully integrated system for performance excellence (integration).

It is at this stage that results improve significantly and consistently due to the concentration of efforts on the critical success factors of the organization. While many refer to the Criteria for Performance Excellence as a framework for improvement (and the Criteria do require continuous improvement of everything you do), they are most beneficial as a framework for development of an integrated system to achieve performance excellence. Effective integration is the turning point that puts an organization on the path to excellence.

Applying ADLI to an Individual Process

While the Criteria provide a framework for assessment and improvement at an organizational or enterprise level, the journey embedded within the ADLI scoring dimensions can be applied to any process. Imagine you are in charge of measuring customer satisfaction (Item 3.1b). How would ADLI inform the steps you take to establish an excellent customer satisfaction measurement system?

- Develop an approach (A) that is systematic and effective. To accomplish this you might develop your own survey, or contract with a third-party firm to acquire well-researched surveys that provide access to normative data and benchmarks.
- Deploy (D) the approach by beginning to administer these surveys to some of your key customer groups at defined intervals or after key transactions have been completed. Over time you may expand the number of customer groups or transactions that are measured using each survey.
- Evaluate the approach so you can learn (L) how to improve it. To begin, perhaps you would evaluate the response rate for each survey. Are enough surveys being returned? Is the sampling method providing a population of returned surveys that is representative of the customer group as a whole and each key segment? You might also evaluate the survey itself. Do customers understand the survey questions and response options? Are there any other questions that should be included on the survey or any to eliminate? Are there better ways to analyze and use the survey data? Are there any best practices you could learn from and adapt to meet your needs?
- Align customer satisfaction measurement with your organization's needs and with other approaches to create an integrated (I) system. For example, you might use the results of customer surveys to inform other processes such as strategic planning (2.1a), product or service innovation (3.2a), service recovery (3.2b), employee performance appraisal (5.2a), employee training (5.2b), or work process management (6.1b).

ADLI Informs Feedback and Scoring

As previously stated, the ADLI evaluation factors are used by examiners to develop feedback comments and scores for each item. The feedback report developed by examiners and provided to applicants includes:

- Executive summary highlighting key themes, areas of strength, and opportunities for improvement

- Feedback comments (typically 3–5 strength comments and 3–5 opportunity for improvement comments) for each of the 17 items in the Criteria
- Percentage scores (0–100%) for each Item
- A total score (0–1000 points)

Before discussing point values and explaining the scoring guidelines in detail, it is important to address the subject of points and awards and their place in the overall process of improvement.

IS THIS JUST ABOUT WINNING AN AWARD?

You may be thinking that this road map is an approach for winning awards. It is not. It is designed as a means to improve organizational performance. However, awards are often the initial impetus for organizations to get involved with the Baldrige process and they provide a way to publicly recognize the accomplishments of an organization's workforce. Rest assured, no organization will ever become Baldrige-worthy without a serious commitment to the achievement of excellence. Almost half (450 of 1,000) of the total points awarded are for Category 7 results. You cannot just look good (effective approaches), you must actually be good (exemplary results). The purpose of the approaches in Categories 1–6 is to create a system that is able to consistently produce exemplary results.

If you start out primarily interested in winning the award but end up becoming an excellent organization with role model results, there is nothing wrong with that. The reason for the strategy provided here is to provide a manageable way for organizations to get on the path and stage the journey. A clear understanding of the scoring guidelines and structure of the Criteria requirements will enable you to manage the journey most effectively. If it also happens to enhance your award status, that is a plus, but not our purpose.

Points Identify Milestones in the Journey

Baldrige and state award decisions are typically not made on the basis of points. While organizations should not focus on improving their score, points are one way to track progress toward becoming a world-class or Baldrige-worthy organization.

During an evaluation, examiners assign a score from 0–100% for each item based on the Strengths and OFIs (opportunities for improvement) identified by the examiner team. The percentage score is multiplied by the point value of the item to determine the points awarded. For example, if an organization receives a score of 50% for Item 1.1 (which is worth 70 points), 35 points would be awarded. Extrapolating further, if you received 50% for every item, your total score would be 500 points.

After completing their first assessment, most organizations score between 200 and 300 points. Most Baldrige recipients score between 700 and 800 points. While organizations should not focus on improving their score, one way to think of the journey to excellence is as a multi-year process to make the improvements required for your scores to increase to 700 points. By doing so, you become a world-class, Baldrige-worthy organization. Even though almost half the points are for results, the focus of the journey is on improvement of the processes in Categories 1–6 that produce those results.

To reach the level where examiners will award you a score of approximately 700 points you will need to meet the requirements of the 50–65% scoring band (refer to Table 2.1) for all approaches in Categories 1–6. This scoring band requires that you have effective, systematic approaches (A) to meet the overall (not the multiple) requirements of each item. These approaches need to be well-deployed (D), to have gone through multiple cycles of fact-based, systematic evaluation to improve their efficiency and effectiveness (L), and to be aligned with overall organizational needs (I).

A score of 65% for each item in Categories 1–6 nets you about 350 points. If you do likewise in Category 7, achieving 65% for each results item, this nets about 300 points. This puts you at 650 points total. If you can break out of the 50–65% scoring band for just one or two items that are of strategic importance to your organization, you will be approaching 700 points and will likely be Baldrige-worthy.

In other words, by focusing on systematic, effective approaches for each of the 28 areas to address that meet the overall requirements of Categories 1–6, an organization can become nearly Baldrige-worthy. Along the way you use the opportunities identified through self-assessment and award program feedback reports to continually improve these key approaches.

One of the benefits of an initial focus on the 50–65% scoring band is that after you have defined and deployed systematic approaches that meet the overall requirements, most of the opportunities you receive in subsequent feedback reports will focus on improvements relative to the multiple requirements that are of most importance based on the key factors for your organization. In other words, the examiners will attempt to identify those multiple requirements that are most important for your organization to address.

How Good Do We Need to Be?

At some point, leaders must ask the legitimate question. How good must our organization be in each of the processes required by Categories 1–6? The answer is that it depends. At a minimum, an excellent organization should meet the overall requirements for all 28 areas to address. Going beyond that for any one item or area to address will depend on your strategy. Baldrige recipients typically score near the top of the 50–65% scoring band for every item in Categories 1–6 and achieve the 70–85% band for a few items of strategic importance.

To illustrate this concept, a company that competes through the continuous release of new products (think 3M) might invest in its product design process (6.1a) to the level that they will achieve a score of 70–85% for this item. A company whose strategy is customer loyalty (think Nordstrom) might invest to achieve 70–85% in customer relationship management (3.2b). A company that competes through analytics (think Harrah's Casino) might invest to achieve 70–85% in data analysis (4.1b).

The purpose of this discussion is not to plot a course to maximize your Baldrige score. The intent is to explain that you do not need to achieve the 70–85% scoring band for every one of the processes required by the Criteria to become an excellent organization. You must have effective, systematic approaches to meet overall requirements for every area to address. Beyond that you will invest in further improvement based on your strategy and organizational needs.

Point Values and Scoring Guidelines

Page 3 of the Criteria book lists the point values for each item. The total points available are 1,000. Of these, 450 points are awarded for Category 7 results, and the remaining 550 points are for the approaches in Categories 1–6. The percentage scores awarded for any single item are based on the Scoring Guidelines found in the Criteria booklet. There are two different sets of scoring guidelines. One is the process scoring guidelines for Categories 1–6 and the other is the results scoring guidelines for Category 7.

Table 2.1 summarizes the process scoring guidelines. Note that there are six scoring bands: 0–5%, 10–25%, 30–45%, 50–65%, 70–85%, and 90–100%. As previously stated, the road map begins with design of key approaches that meet the overall requirements. For this reason, the 50–65% scoring band is highlighted in Table 2.1, as this is the initial target when designing your operating model.

Table 2.1 Process scoring guidelines.

Score	Description (for use with Categories 1–6)
0% or 5%	• No systematic approach to item requirements is evident; information is anecdotal. (A) • Little or no deployment of any systematic approach is evident. (D) • An improvement orientation is not evident; improvement is achieved by reacting to problems. (L) • No organizational alignment is evident; individual areas or work units operate independently. (I)
10%, 15%, 20%, or 25%	• The beginning of a systematic approach to the **BASIC** requirements of the item is evident. (A) • The approach is in the early stages of deployment in most areas or work units inhibiting progress in achieving the basic requirements of the item. (D) • Early stages of a transition from reacting to problems to a general improvement orientation are evident. (L) • Approach is aligned with other areas or work units largely through joint problem solving. (I)
30%, 35%, 40%, or 45%	• An effective, systematic approach, responsive to the **BASIC** requirements of the item, is evident. (A) • The approach is deployed, although some areas or work units are in early stages of deployment. (D) • The beginning of a systematic approach to evaluation and improvement of key processes is evident. (L) • Approach is in the early stages of alignment with your basic organizational needs identified in the Organizational Profile and other process items. (I)
50%, 55%, 60%, or 65%	• An effective, systematic approach, responsive to the **OVERALL** requirements of the item, is evident. (A) • The approach is well deployed, although deployment may vary in some areas or work units. (D) • A fact-based, systematic evaluation and improvement process and some organizational learning, including innovation, are in place for improving the efficiency and effectiveness of key processes. (L) • Approach is aligned with overall organizational needs identified in the Organizational Profile and other process items. (I)
70%, 75%, 80%, or 85%	• An effective, systematic approach, responsive to the **MULTIPLE** requirements of the item, is evident. (A) • The approach is well deployed, with no significant gaps. (D) • Fact-based, systematic evaluation and improvement and organizational learning, including innovation, are key management tools; there is clear evidence of refinement as a result of organizational-level analysis and sharing. (L) • Approach is integrated with current and future organizational needs identified in the Organizational Profile and other process items. (I)

(Continued)

Table 2.1 Process scoring guidelines *(continued)*.

Score	Description (for use with Categories 1–6)
90%, 95%, or 100%	• An effective, systematic approach, fully responsive to the multiple requirements of the item, is evident. (A) • The approach is fully deployed without significant weaknesses or gaps in any areas or work units. (D) • Fact-based, systematic evaluation and improvement and organizational learning through innovation are key organization-wide tools; refinement and innovation, backed by analysis and sharing, are evident throughout the organization. (L) • Approach is well integrated with current and future organizational needs identified in the Organizational Profile and other process items. (I)

Differences in ADLI Scoring Guidelines Describe Levels of Maturity

The bottom scoring band (0–5%) in Table 2.1 applies when you have no process and the top band (90–100%) applies when processes are approaching perfection. Since both situations rarely apply, Table 2.2 focuses on the four middle bands. It highlights key differences in ADLI for each successive band.

Once you understand ADLI, the steps in the journey to excellence for each key approach become clear. The challenge arises when an organization's leaders begin reviewing the 200 or more questions without a clear road map. They can become confused and overwhelmed by the number of approaches they think are needed to meet requirements.

Table 2.2 Key differences in ADLI scoring dimensions.

Band	Approach (A)	Deployment (D)	Learning (L)	Integration (I)
10–25%	Systematic approaches to meet basic requirements	Early stages of deployment in most areas or work units	Transition from reacting to problems to a general improvement orientation	Approach is generally aligned with other processes
30–45%	Effective, systematic approaches to meet basic requirements	Approaches are deployed Some areas or units are in early stages	Beginning to systematically evaluate and improve key processes	Approach is aligned with other processes and basic organizational needs

(Continued)

Table 2.2 Key differences in ADLI scoring dimensions *(continued)*.

Band	Approach (A)	Deployment (D)	Learning (L)	Integration (I)
50–65%	Effective, systematic approaches to meet overall requirements	Approaches are well deployed Deployment may vary in some areas or units	Fact-based, systematic evaluation and some organizational learning/innovation used to improve efficiency and effectiveness of key processes	Approach is aligned with other processes and overall organizational needs
70–85%	Effective, systematic approaches to meet multiple requirements	Approaches are well deployed No significant gaps	Fact-based, systematic evaluation and improvement and organizational learning/innovation are key tools and refinement has resulted from organizational-level analysis and sharing	Approach is integrated with other processes and current and future organizational needs

This is why it is essential to develop an understanding of the 28 areas to address within the Criteria and the hierarchy of BOM (basic, overall, multiple) requirements. This will prevent you from becoming overwhelmed and allow you to stage the journey as you learn your way to excellence over time.

BOM (BASIC, OVERALL, MULTIPLE) ALLOW YOU TO STAGE THE JOURNEY

If you review the description of the approach (A) dimension in the scoring guidelines, you will note one key difference in the scoring bands. The 10–25% and 30–45% scoring bands require approaches responsive to the basic requirements. The 50–65% scoring band requires approaches responsive to the overall requirements, and the remaining bands require approaches responsive to the multiple requirements. This hierarchy of requirements (basic, overall, multiple) within each item provides a manageable way to stage the journey for organizations seeking to build an integrated performance excellence system.

Figure 2.1 explains the structure of Item 3.1 in order to provide an example of the hierarchy of approach requirements that include the basic, overall, and multiple level requirements. The Health Care Criteria for Performance Excellence are shown in Figure 2.1, but the language used here is simplified to *customers*. This is the major difference in the three

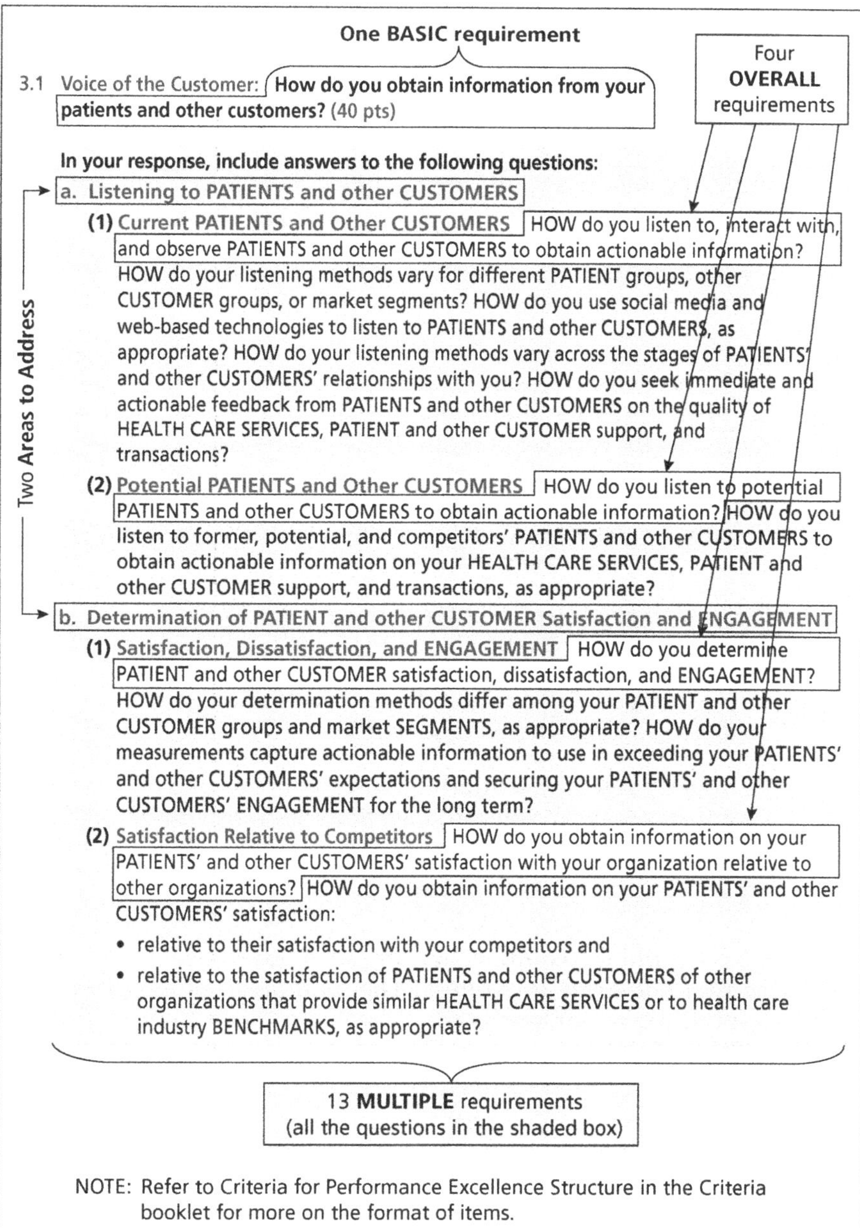

Figure 2.1 Explanation of Item format.

versions of the Criteria. The term *customers* is used in the business, service, and non-profit Criteria. In the Health Care Criteria the terms used are *patients* and *other customers*. In the Education Criteria the terms used are *students* and *stakeholders*.

BASIC – 3.1 is the item level and corresponds to the Basic requirement:

3.1 How do you obtain information from your customers?

OVERALL – The overall requirements are the first, boldfaced question in each set of multiple requirements. In Item 3.1 there are four overall requirements, one for each set of multiple requirements.

3.1a(1) How do you listen to, interact with, and observe customers to obtain actionable information?

3.1a(2) How do you listen to potential customers to obtain actionable information?

3.1b(1) How do you determine customer satisfaction, dissatisfaction, and engagement?

3.1b(2) How do you obtain information on your customers' satisfaction with your organization relative to other organizations?

MULTIPLE – Multiple requirements are all of the detailed questions within the four sub-areas to address. The 13 individual questions that define the multiple requirements for Item 3.1 in the 2015–2016 Criteria are shown below. The first question in each set is boldfaced. These four questions represent the overall requirements as described previously.

3.1a(1) Current Customers

How do you listen to, interact with, and observe customers to obtain actionable information?

How do your listening methods vary for different customer groups, or market segments?

How do you use social media and web-based technologies to listen to customers, as appropriate?

How do your listening methods vary across the stages of customers' relationships with you?

How do you seek immediate and actionable feedback from customers on the quality of services, customer support, and transactions?

3.1a(2) Potential Customers

How do you listen to potential customers to obtain actionable information?

How do you listen to former, potential, and competitors' customers to obtain actionable information on your services, customer support, and transactions, as appropriate?

3.1b(1) Satisfaction, Dissatisfaction, and Engagement

How do you determine customer satisfaction, dissatisfaction, and engagement?

How do your determination methods differ among your customer groups and market segments, as appropriate?

How do your measurements capture actionable information to use in exceeding your customers' expectations and securing your customers' engagement for the long term?

3.1b(2) Satisfaction Relative to Competitors

How do you obtain information on your customers' satisfaction with your organization relative to other organizations?

How do you obtain information on your customers' satisfaction:

- relative to their satisfaction with your competitors and
- relative to the satisfaction of customers of organizations that provide similar services or to industry benchmarks, as appropriate?

As you read the detailed multiple requirements, it is not surprising that establishing systematic processes that fully respond to all 13 questions within sub-areas 3.1a(1) through 3.1b(2) can be overwhelming. When you multiply this by 12 to include all approach items in Categories 1–6, you can understand why the first steps in the journey appear so daunting to organizations. The areas to address and overall requirements provide a way to manage this complexity.

AREAS TO ADDRESS ARE THE BUILDING BLOCKS FOR PERFORMANCE EXCELLENCE

Note in Figure 2.1 that Item 3.1 includes two areas to address.

3.1a Listen to Customers

3.1b Determine Customer Satisfaction and Engagement

Following is a listing of the 28 areas to address in Categories 1–6 of the Criteria. Each typically includes two to five overall requirements. These serve as the building blocks for design of an organization's performance excellence system.

1.1a Vision, Values, and Mission
1.1b Communication and Organizational Performance
1.2a Organizational Governance
1.2b Legal and Ethical Behavior
1.2c Societal Responsibilities
2.1a Strategy Development Process
2.1b Strategic Objectives
2.2a Action Plan Development and Deployment
2.2b Action Plan Modification
3.1a Customer Listening
3.1b Determination of Customer Satisfaction and Engagement
3.2a Product/Service Offerings and Customer Support
3.2b Customer Relationships
4.1a Performance Measurement
4.1b Performance Analysis and Review
4.1c Performance Improvement
4.2a Organizational Knowledge

4.2b Data, Information, and Information Technology
5.1a Workforce Capability and Capacity
5.1b Workforce Climate
5.2a Workforce Engagement and Performance
5.2b Workforce and Leader Development
6.1a Product/Service and Process Design
6.1b Process Management
6.1c Innovation Management
6.2a Process Efficiency and Effectiveness
6.2b Supply-Chain Management
6.2c Safety and Emergency Preparedness

The road map detailed in Chapter 3 recommends building your performance excellence system based on the key approaches your organization uses to meet the overall requirements for each of these areas to address. This will typically number about 30 key approaches, a manageable number for an organization when beginning to design a performance excellence system.

For each key approach, identify an owner who is responsible to develop a one-page graphical summary of the key approach. Each key approach is deployed and systematically evaluated and improved over time. Feedback from award programs is used as one key input to these cycles of improvement. You learn the way to excellence over time.

Any organization that is serious about excellence should have the willingness and the capacity to define and manage approximately 30 key approaches that are required for performance excellence. As explained in the next section, by following this process you will also reduce the time and effort required to develop applications, prepare for site visits, and effectively use feedback reports.

Using Key Approaches in Application and Feedback Review Processes

Starting with a focus on the definition and management of approximately 30 key approaches that correspond to the areas to address in Categories 1–6 simplifies the process for application development and feedback. Once key approaches are identified and defined, they can be used in several ways:

- Graphical summaries of each key approach provide the majority of the content (figures) included in the application for Categories 1–6. The remainder of the application content in Categories 1–6 is the text that explains these key approaches and describes how they meet many of the multiple requirements.

- One-page summaries can be shared in order to deploy key approaches. For example, managers may receive training on the key approaches, or participate in a series of lunch-and-learn sessions during which the key approaches are reviewed and explained.
- During the site visit, when examiners ask about a key approach, employees can use the key approach documents as an aid when explaining the process. Site visits do not require employees to pass a memory test. The summaries of key approaches are very effective aids when used appropriately during the site visit.
- When the feedback report is received, each OFI (Opportunity for Improvement) can be "assigned" to one of the key approaches.
- Each key approach is evaluated and improved by its owner at least twice per year using available data. This will include OFIs either identified through self-assessment (in July) or included in the award program feedback report (January). This ensures systematic cycles of evaluation and improvement for each key approach. Page 2 of each key approach document is used to record the history of improvements made in the approach as a result of these semi-annual evaluation and improvement sessions. This provides examiners with evidence of cycles of systematic evaluation and improvement.

During these evaluations of key approaches, any OFI received in the feedback report that is related to ADLI of overall approaches must be addressed. It is likely that once key approaches have been established, most of the feedback received by an organization will be related to deployment gaps or to the multiple requirements. An OFI related to multiple requirements should be evaluated in terms of its importance to the organization's key goals and customer requirements. For each multiple-level OFI, the examiner team will have evaluated and determined the most important of the multiple requirements that are not addressed, typically based on their alignment with the key factors of the organization.

The owner of each key approach will receive this feedback and can decide what changes (if any) to make in each key approach to meet these multiple requirements. You may decide that some multiple requirements are not essential to the success and sustainability of your organization and therefore not worth the effort. This is ok. You do not need to achieve the 70–85% band for every item in order to be an excellent organization or to be worthy of the Baldrige award. Baldrige award recipients receive feedback reports with fifty or more OFIs, so they are not perfect. But to ensure success and sustainability, an organization should aim to achieve a level of maturity in all of its key approaches that merit a score at the top of the 50–65% band with effective and systematic approaches to meet the overall requirements for each area to address.

AWARD PROGRAM A SOURCE OF COMPREHENSIVE, OBJECTIVE FEEDBACK

By focusing on ADLI for the key approaches in Categories 1–6 as described previously, you have a good chance to achieve some level of recognition from your state award within one to two years. The feedback received from your state award program can be used over several years to help your leaders mature and integrate the individual elements of your performance excellence system and address those multiple requirements of importance to your organization's strategy and key requirements. Within three to four years you are likely to be well positioned for the Baldrige Award. Even if you do not win the Baldrige, you will have become a much better organization for having embarked on the journey described here.

It is recommended that you think of the state and national award programs in a different light. You are using the Criteria as a blueprint to design and implement your organization's operating model for performance excellence. Viewed this way, the award program is simply an inexpensive source of comprehensive, annual, objective feedback on the progress of that effort. Examiners typically spend 500 to 1,000 hours in the evaluation of an application. This means the feedback report they produce is conservatively worth well over $100,000 in examiner time and can be acquired for much less than that amount.

If you are committed to using the Criteria to design your organization's operating model, then annual use of your state's Baldrige-based award program provides inexpensive feedback on the effectiveness of your model. The awards you receive along the way are simply a happy by-product of this process and provide a means to recognize and congratulate your employees for milestones achieved at different points in this journey.

Use the award process;
don't let the process use you.

Apply, Improve, Repeat

The best users of state award programs are repeat applicants. Every year (or at least every other year) they develop and submit an application and act on the feedback received. In fact, given the time and effort required to develop and submit a first application, it makes almost no sense from a cost/benefit perspective to apply just once. Instead of developing a single application, establish an efficient process that allows you to:

- Define and deploy key approaches to meet the overall requirements for each area to address in Categories 1-6.
- Use the documentation of key approaches as the basis for development of an application.
- Use key approach documents to deploy these processes, to prepare the workforce for site visit, and as aids during site visit.
- Assign each OFI from the feedback report to the appropriate key approach owners.
- Consider each OFI from the feedback report as one input in the semi-annual evaluation and improvement of key approaches.

The process summarized here is detailed in the next chapter.

3

Turn-by-turn Directions for the Journey

The multi-year journey to excellence is navigated by using a systematic process to design, deploy, evaluate, and improve the key approaches that comprise your organization's Baldrige-based operating model for excellence. The road map for this journey recommends annual use of your state award program to obtain inexpensive external feedback that can be used to refine your organization's operating model. The recommended process to design and refine your operating model over time is summarized in Figure 3.1 as CAP-Do,[8] which is how the PDCA cycle is often applied in practice.

The key steps in the CAP-Do process are:

- **CHECK** – The purpose of the Check step is to identify opportunities for improvement. This is accomplished by evaluating the effectiveness of approximately 30 key approaches twice each year, during July and January. Sources of input to these semi-annual evaluations are the opportunities for improvement (OFIs) identified through self-assessment (July) and those included in feedback reports (January).
- **ACT** – The Act in CAP-Do (and PDCA) is a decision step. Key approach owners prioritize identified opportunities and decide what actions (if any) will be taken to address them. They must address each OFI that relates to requirements at the basic or overall level. They may choose not to address some multiple level OFIs, or those related to deployment of an approach to groups that are considered unimportant to organizational success.
- **PLAN** – Document the improvements that will be made in the approach and the action plan to implement changes in the process. Owners update their key approach documentation to reflect the changes made and record these in the history of improvement.

- **Do** – Implement improvements in key approaches. This often involves communication and training of staff, and should include observation of the modified process to ensure the changes have been deployed. Observation also allows the owner to gather input and identify additional opportunities for improvement of the key approach.

Prior to initiating the CAP-Do cycle described in Figure 3.1, it is important to complete a number of actions in year one of the journey to establish a foundation of key approaches, and the structure, process, and accountabilities for their ongoing evaluation and improvement. The process that is established must enable the systematic evaluation and improvement of key approaches, and should integrate with an efficient and effective process to develop and submit award applications, host site visits, and use the feedback reports received from the award program.

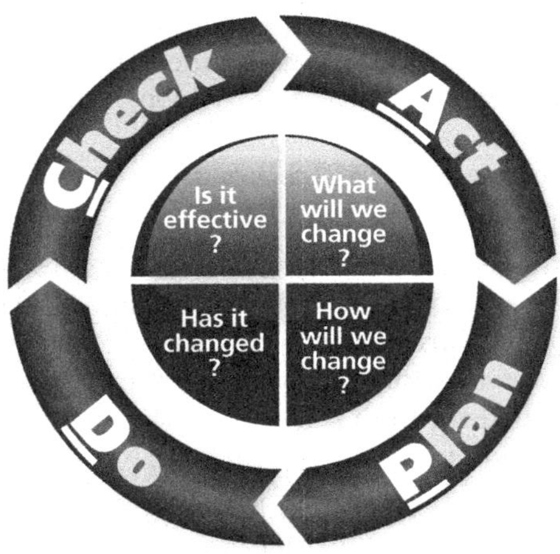

Figure 3.1 CAP-Do process for systematic evaluation and improvement of key approaches.

YEAR ONE: ESTABLISH THE FOUNDATION, STRUCTURE, AND ACCOUNTABILITIES

The steps to be completed in year one are described in this section and organized into the following phases:

- Get started
- Get organized
- Identify key approaches
- Document key approaches

These steps provide the foundation and structure for the annual, recurring cycle that includes:

- Application development
- Site visit
- Feedback
- Improvement

Following are a specific set of turn-by-turn directions for year one and beyond. The 35 steps described in this chapter are detailed by design. They are intended to provide organizations with clear directions for the journey as they chart a course for their own organization.

Get Started

1. *State Award Programs:* Find your state award program (go to www.baldrigepe.org/alliance for links to state award programs). Ask your program for information about their offerings. Most offer some type of tiered awards (e.g., Bronze, Silver, and Gold) and various approaches to help you get started. In 2015 the Baldrige Program introduced the *Baldrige Excellence Builder* as a starting point for organizational learning and assessment. It is a free resource that includes only the overall requirements. Some state award programs offer an abbreviated assessment based on these requirements. Virtually all state award programs will also offer training. Senior leaders need to develop a basic understanding of the Criteria, award program, and processes in order to implement the approach being described here.
2. *Organizational Profile:* Review and discuss key questions in the Organizational Profile to become familiar with these concepts and define the key factors for your organization. Early in the process, leaders should discuss and ensure clarity around key factors that define your Organizational Profile, illustrated in Table 3.1.

Table 3.1 Key factors in an organizational profile.

Key Factors	Identified in...	Have implications for...
Mission, Vision, Values	P.1a(2)	Item 1.1
Key products and services	P.1a(1)	Item 6.1
Key customer groups and/or market segments	P.1b(2)	Item 3.2a(3)
Key requirements for each customer group or segment	P.1b(2)	Item 3.2a(1), 6.1
Key strategic challenges, advantages, and opportunities	P.2b	Items 2.1, 6.1c
Core competencies	P.1a(2)	Items 2.1a(4), 6.1

NOTE: Some state-award programs offer feedback on the five-page Organizational Profile as an entry-level step.

Get Organized

3. *Category Teams:* Establish six cross-functional Category teams aligned with Categories 1–6. Each team includes a member of senior leadership who serves as sponsor for the Category. For example, your CEO is often the sponsor for Category 1, your VP Planning for Category 2, your HR leader for Category 5, and so on. In addition to the sponsor, each Category team should include three to five other individuals who are selected based on their roles in the organization. These are individuals who are likely to be identified as owners of the key approaches within each Category. For small organizations, it often makes sense to combine Categories (e.g., 1 and 5, 2 and 4, 3 and 6) and have just three sponsors and three teams.
4. *Application Development Team:* Identify an individual to serve as lead for the application development process. Ideally this is someone within the organization who has multiple years of experience as a state or national examiner, and who is well-positioned relative to the senior leadership team. This person will identify two to three other individuals to assist with writing the application and the compilation of Category 7 results. The application lead and his/her delegates should attend each of the self-assessment sessions and all Category team meetings.
5. *Kick-off Session:* Conduct a kick-off meeting with sponsors, Category teams, and the application development team. This is used to educate leaders on the Baldrige framework and clarify the approach being taken and the expectations for the self-assessment

that will occur in subsequent meetings. During this meeting, a review of overall requirements can be used to validate the initial assignment of individuals to Category teams. The session concludes with assignment of pre-work for the Category teams. This is typically to review the Criteria for their assigned items and reflect on the key approaches being used by the organization to meet those requirements.

Identify Key Approaches

6. *Key Approach Identification Workshops:* Conduct three workshops to complete a self-assessment relative to the requirements of the Criteria. The multiple requirements are used during these workshops to educate leaders and inform the assessment. At the conclusion of the assessment for each item, the key deliverables are to agree on (1) the key approach that is used to meet the overall requirements for each area to address and (2) the individual who will serve as owner or single point accountable (SPA) for each one of these key approaches. These workshops also serve to educate leaders on the Criteria requirements, identify possible opportunities for improvement of key approaches, identify key results that correspond to the approaches, and identify the process or subject matter experts who will support key approach owners in completing their assignments.

Due to the natural alignment between approaches in different Categories, it is recommended you combine Categories when completing this initial self-assessment. As illustrated in Table 3.2, one workshop can be used to complete the assessment of Categories 2 and 4, another for Categories 1 and 5, and a third for Categories 3 and 6. The pairing of categories is based on the typical alignment of processes and results within each one. Senior leaders should attend all three of these sessions, while other Category team members attend only the sessions they are assigned. The application development team should attend all sessions and should develop a log of opportunities for improvement (OFIs) that are identified during the self-assessment process.

NOTE: OP refers to Organizational Profile in Table 3.2.

Table 3.2 Key approach identification workshops.

Workshop 1	Workshop 2	Workshop 3
Category 2 • OP: P.2a(1-2), P.2b • Approach Items 2.1, 2.2 • Results Item 7.4b	Category 1 • OP: P.1a(2), P.1a(5), P.1b(1) • Approach Items 1.1, 1.2 • Results Item 7.4a	Category 3 • OP: P.1b(2) • Approach Items 3.1, 3.2 • Results Item 7.2
Category 4 • OP: P.2a(3), P.2c • Approach Items 4.1, 4.2 • Results Item 7.5	Category 5 • OP: P.1a(3) • Approach Items 5.1, 5.2 • Results Item 7.3	Category 6 • OP: P.1a(1), P.1a(4), P.1b(3), P.2c • Approach Items 6.1, 6.2 • Results Item 7.1

During each key approach identification workshop, the results items related to the Categories being covered are also addressed, to the extent possible at this time. In addition, if senior leaders have discussed and developed preliminary responses to Organizational Profile (OP) questions, these can be summarized and reviewed, or provided as pre-work for the sessions.

Based on the completed assessment, the application development team develops a summary of the key approaches and owners for each one. This will cover all 28 areas to address in Categories 1–6. However, the number of key approaches identified will vary in every organization. You may choose to group some areas together and/or sub-divide others. For example, you might combine 2.1b Strategic Objectives and 2.2a(6) Projections into a single key approach. In other cases, it makes sense to sub-divide a single area to address into more than one overall approach. A common example is 3.2b, which includes both Relationship Management [3.2b(1)] and Complaint Management [3.2b(2)]. The identification of key approaches will vary for every organization, but in most cases no more than 35 are needed to cover all areas to address in Categories 1–6. For smaller organizations, fewer key approaches are often sufficient to adequately respond to requirements. In a small company, a single process can address several overall requirements across different items very effectively.

7. *Follow-Up Workshop:* Reconvene the Category sponsors, key approach owners, and identified process or subject matter experts. The objectives of this workshop are to:

   - Review and confirm the list of key approaches, owners, and experts.
   - Reconsider the assignment of sponsors and the membership of Category teams based on the identification of key approach owners and process experts.

- Clarify the accountabilities of Category sponsors and key approach owners.
- Provide templates and tools to accelerate the documentation of key approaches.
- Review the timeline for completion of key approach documentation.
- Revisit and commit to the larger purpose for this effort.
- Review and agree on a high-level change plan for communication and management of this effort.

Change Management

The last point in the list of objectives in Step 7 identifies the need for senior leaders to be thoughtful about the change management implications for the work they are doing. By the time they arrive at this point in the process (Step 7), senior leaders should have a plan to communicate what they are doing with key stakeholders and to integrate the work requirements of the effort into the organization's accountability management structures. The following brief detour from the description of the year-one process provides recommended approaches for doing so.

Stakeholder management: Because of the importance of the work being done by senior leaders and key approach owners, and the likely interest in this effort among staff and other key stakeholders, it is recommended that senior leaders and key approach owners conduct a series of discussions with staff and key stakeholders. These discussions are used to explain the journey the organization is beginning, to clarify the purpose of this effort, and to answer questions and listen in order to understand their concerns. At this point in the process, the leaders will have enough of a sense of the direction they are taking with identification of key approaches to communicate effectively about the process and to clarify where assistance will be needed from staff and stakeholders in upcoming steps to define or design key approaches.

KA owner is SPA: During key approach identification workshops, an individual will be assigned to serve as key approach (KA) owner or single point accountable (SPA) for each of the 30 or so key approaches identified. The assignment of a single point accountable (SPA) is based on my experience that unless one person is identified as the accountable party for something, then no one is accountable for it. In a few cases, the SPA for a key approach will also be the Category sponsor. In most cases, a direct report of leadership will be the most appropriate KA owner. As SPA, the KA owner is expected to define and manage the process for each key approach, including semi-annual evaluation and improvement cycles. Depending on the scope and complexity of the process, the KA owner may form a team that includes process or subject matter experts who will assist in the design and ongoing improvement of the key approach. The KA owner is accountable, though team members or delegates are usually responsible for doing much of the work.

If no one person is accountable, nobody is accountable.

Accountability management: To create clear expectations and accountabilities, it is recommended that you modify the individual performance goals of those senior leaders who serve as sponsors, and those individuals who serve as key approach owners. The individual goals included in their annual performance evaluations should reflect the work required for successful completion of these activities. If the work required of key approach owners is not prioritized and integrated into the performance management system of the organization, there is a significant risk that managers will view the "Baldrige work" as separate from and less important than their "real work." In this case it is unlikely that progress will occur at the rate and level needed to achieve and sustain performance excellence. Following are examples of recommended accountabilities for sponsors and key approach owners.

Category sponsor is responsible for the following:

- Review key approach documentation and provide feedback to key approach owners.
- Review key approach improvement plans twice each year after owners complete their semi-annual evaluation/improvement.
- Monitor progress by key approach owners and report on status to senior leadership.
- Work with other members of senior leadership to integrate key approaches, address issues or barriers, and ensure allocation of resources as needed.
- Provide the application team with the information needed to develop an award application.
- Prepare for and participate in the site visit.
- Provide input to improve the overarching process that is used to manage key approaches and the organization's performance excellence system as a whole.

Key Approach (KA) owners are responsible for the following:

- DOCUMENT: Work with process experts to document one-page summaries for each key approach. The KA document serves to either *define* a current approach, or *design* a new process when no approach exists to meet overall requirements.
- EVALUATE and IMPROVE: Convene semi-annual KA review meetings (January and July) to evaluate key approaches, identify and prioritize opportunities, and implement improvements. These meetings serve as the primary method for systematic, fact-based evaluation and improvement of key approaches to achieve and sustain performance excellence. Steps follow the CAP-Do model in Figure 3.1 and typically include:
  1. Gather and analyze the information needed to evaluate key approaches. Sources of data/information used during evaluations include the Criteria for Performance Excellence that defines the requirements for key approaches, performance data for measures of the effectiveness and efficiency of key approaches, and the OFIs identified via self-assessment or included in award program feedback reports.
     - In July: After the application is submitted in May, use the OFIs self-identified during the application development process as input to the July evaluation.
     - In January: After the feedback report is received in December, use the OFIs received from the award program as a key input to the January evaluation.
  2. Involve process experts and other staff as needed in the semi-annual evaluations used to identify opportunities and improve key approaches.
  3. Plan and implement improvements in key approaches.
  4. Deploy changes in key approaches to staff and key stakeholders, including communication, training, and observation as needed.
- SUPPORT: Work with the application development team as requested to:
  1. Update key approach documentation, including the history of improvement. All KA summaries must be updated before application development begins in February.
  2. Provide other information as needed to develop the award application.

3. Prepare staff and key stakeholders and participate in the site visit.
4. Provide input to improve the process used to manage key approaches.

The preceding section on Change Management provided recommendations for communicating with staff about the work being undertaken to design the organization's operating model and ensuring this work is integrated into existing approaches for accountability management. The description of Key Approach owner responsibilities also serves as a useful introduction to Step 8 in the year-one process.

Document Key Approaches

8. *Develop Key Approach Documents:* The key approach (KA) owner serves as the single point accountable with responsibility to ensure that each key approach is defined, deployed, and managed for improvement.

   KA owners enlist process experts to develop a one- or two-page summary for each key approach. These KA summaries serve as documentation of the organization's operating model for performance excellence. These KA documents are:

   - The focal point for application development. The application development team uses the KA documents updated after the January cycle of KA evaluation and improvement as the basis for development of the next application.
   - Used to deploy key approaches.
   - Used as interview aids during site visits.
   - The means to assign OFIs to KAs (self-assessment OFIs in July; feedback report OFIs in January), which are then used as one input into KA evaluation and improvement.
   - The means to document changes in processes resulting from the semi-annual cycles of evaluation and improvement for each KA.
   - The means to document the "history of improvement" for the key approach and provide examiners with evidence of evaluation and improvement cycles for each KA.

   Each KA document should be a separate file, treated as a controlled document and stored on an appropriate repository such as a shared drive or SharePoint site on the organization's internal network. You may wish to limit access or edit capabilities for these documents or include revision dates, though this is not mandatory. It is suggested that the file name of the document identify the item, the key approach, and the owner. For example, a KA document might have the file name:

1.1a Leadership System (John Doe)

An example template for KA documentation (Tables 4.7, 4.8 and 4.9) is provided on the last few pages of Chapter 4.

NOTE: Companion pieces to this book provide detailed templates and tools to guide KA owners and accelerate the initial documentation of key approaches.

Sponsors and KA owners should consider the following during the development of key approach documentation.

Page one of KA document

Definition or Design: KA documents can be as little as two pages. To develop page one, you document what the organization currently does in a clear, summarized format. If there is not a current approach used by the organization, then the KA owner will design a process to meet requirements and document this in the KA summary. Page one will typically take one of these forms:

- Table to summarize a list of methods that collectively comprise a key approach.
- Process definition (5x5)[9] summarizing the five major steps in the process, and the five sub-steps within each major step.
- Process map, in a swim lane or flow chart format. Figure 3.2 is an example of a swim lane map.
- Graphical depiction of a closed-loop process. The CAP-Do model in Figure 3.1 is an example of a closed-loop process.

Experience has shown that 5x5 process definition templates are useful for documenting key approaches. Following are some advantages of the 5x5 method for definition of key approaches.

- It is a quick and simple way to define a process.
- It provides an appropriate level of detail, even when defining very complex processes.
- It is well-suited to management processes, which are often difficult to map using swim lane or flowchart diagrams.
- It can include evaluation and improvement as step #5 for each key approach, to build in cycles of evaluation and improvement.

- It makes it easy to summarize the key approach within an award application in abbreviated form by including only the five major steps from the KA document.

Observation: It is recommended that key approach owners and/or experts "go to the Gemba"[10] to observe the process in action, or interview those who perform the process. It is also useful to review each of the key approach summaries with stakeholders in order to validate its accuracy.

First Sponsor Review and Benchmarking: After the current approach is defined or a proposed approach is designed, the KA owner should review the draft key approach with the Category sponsor. It is at this time that the sponsor, KA owner, and process experts should "benchmark" their approaches by reviewing the applications of Baldrige recipient organizations (available on the Baldrige web site). This is useful to identify best practices and improve both the content and presentation of the approach summary. But it is recommended that you not look at the key approaches of others until you have defined your own. The danger of looking at others before this point is that you might end up with your key approaches being defined as slightly different versions of somebody else's. Should this occur for too many key approaches, it can make buy-in and commitment to the process more difficult.

KA Check-in: It is often helpful to conduct a half-day check-in meeting with key approach owners. The purpose of this meeting is to review the status of the effort and allow owners to share their learnings from the work being done to define/design and document key approaches. This provides an opportunity to identify and resolve any issues in KA documentation and to clarify that owners are expected to develop a history of improvement for each key approach. This will be completed on page two of the KA document.

Page two of KA document

Page two involves briefly documenting the "history of improvement" for the approach as illustrated in Table 3.3. Once the key approach currently in use has been documented, it is relatively easy to identify the changes that have been made in the process during the past few years (e.g., 2011–2015). The rest of the history will be developed over time, as a result of the semi-annual cycles of evaluation and improvement that occur twice each year, in January and July.

Table 3.3 Documentation of improvement history.

Date	Improvements Implemented
When did the evaluation occur?	*What improvements or changes were made in the process?*
2011	
2012	
2013	
2014	
2015	
January 2016	
July 2016	

Second Sponsor Review: After key approach owners finalize the KA summary documents, including both process definition and history of improvement, the Category sponsor should meet again with each KA owner to review the documentation. This is a final checkpoint prior to full review by all senior leaders. During this meeting the sponsors should also ensure that KA owners have validated existing approaches or are preparing to pilot any new key approaches that were not previously in operation.

9. *Finalize Key Approach Documents:* Senior leaders review and approve the KA summaries for all 30 or so key approaches. This is often best accomplished by conducting three half-day sessions. This allows approximately 20 to 30 minutes per key approach for detailed review and discussion before each one is considered final.

   Throughout the process described in Steps 8–9, KA owners will identify numerous opportunities for improvement. Some OFIs will be addressed immediately through definition and deployment of their key approach. Others may require more time or resources than are possible at this stage. These are shared with the application lead and logged in a spreadsheet (OFI Log) for later review and action.

10. *Deploy Key Approaches:* KA owners complete the work required to finalize and deploy key approaches. This may include simple forms of communication and training, such as lunch-and-learn sessions with staff. It may also require documentation of detailed procedures for key process steps, development of standard work, surveys or other tools, and so on. In cases where the key approach was not previously in operation and has been designed, this

would likely involve a process to pilot, evaluate, and refine the approach before full deployment.

11. *KA Evaluation and Improvement:* Once key approaches are documented and deployed, a half-day session with KA owners is recommended to clarify accountabilities (which should be included in their individual performance goals) for owners to complete semi-annual evaluation and improvement of key approaches. This half-day session should train KA owners on:

    - The organization's continuous improvement (CI) model.
    - Effective methods and measures for evaluation of key approaches.
    - The recommended process for semi-annual evaluation and improvement meetings.

    Step 26 provides a detailed explanation of the recommended process for evaluation of key approaches in order to ensure KA evaluation and improvement sessions are systematic and fact-based.

    As follow-up to this half-day session, KA owners develop the methods and/or measures needed to prepare for the first semi-annual evaluation and improvement cycle. Category sponsors review these plans and ensure appropriate preparation for KA evaluation meetings at least one month prior to the first evaluation and improvement meetings.

Upon completion of Step 11, the organization will have developed the documentation of key approaches that comprise its performance excellence system and be prepared for the annual recurring cycle that includes application development, the award process, and semi-annual key approach evaluation and improvement.

YEAR TWO AND BEYOND

Table 3.4 provides a summary of an annual recurring cycle. Four work streams are identified to illustrate how the process integrates the evaluation and improvement of key approaches with application development, the award process cycle, and opportunities for development of leaders.

Table 3.4 The annual cycle.

Work stream	Q1 January–March	Q2 April–June	Q3 July–September	Q4 October–December
Key Approach Evaluation and Improvement	Evaluate and improve key approaches (use feedback report OFIs) Update KA summaries Sponsors review KA status	Leadership Team reviews OFI log of self-identified opportunities	Evaluate and improve key approaches (use self-identified OFIs) Update KA summaries Support efforts to prepare for site visit Sponsors review KA status	Leadership Team reviews feedback report and assignment of OFIs to KA owners Update annual goals of Category sponsors, KA owners, and process experts
Application Development	Application Development Team (ADT) uses KA summaries to develop application drafts for review by leaders, KA owners Document self-identified opportunities in OFI log	ADT finalize and submit application Debrief application development process	Share updated KA summaries to prepare the organization for site visit	Receive and review feedback report Assign each OFI in the feedback report to the appropriate KA owner(s)
Award Process	Attend award ceremony (for prior year)		Prepare for and host site visit Debrief the site visit	Awards announced
Leadership Development	Identify leaders to serve as examiners	Selected leaders trained as examiners Attend Baldrige Quest for Excellence	Leaders serve as examiners Attend Baldrige Regional Conference	

NOTE: By having a handful of employees within the organization serve as state or national award examiners, you will develop the internal expertise needed to effectively support this process. Depending on the experience and Criteria knowledge of these individuals, you may still find that some steps require the assistance of knowledgeable external consultants.

Q1: During Q1 each year, KA owners complete an evaluation of key approaches using OFIs from the feedback report, plan and implement improvements, and update the KA summary documents to reflect these changes. Sponsors meet with their KA owners to review the status of all key approaches and understand what improvements are being implemented. The application development team uses the updated KA documents to develop the main body of the application, circulate it for review, and make revisions. As you develop the application, a number of additional OFIs will be self-identified and should be logged. Hopefully you will also be attending your state's award ceremony based on the prior year's application. These ceremonies are held at different times in each state but typically occur either during Q4 or Q1. The example in Table 3.4 places this event in Q1.

Q2: During Q2, the Application Development Team (ADT) will finalize and submit your application. At the conclusion of this effort, the process is debriefed since you continually seek ways to be more effective and efficient in everything you do. Some current or future leaders should be selected to serve as examiners for either your state or the national award program. Over time you should aim for multiple leaders and managers to develop examiner-level knowledge and skills. Another development opportunity is for leaders to attend the Baldrige Quest for Excellence conference held each year in conjunction with the Baldrige Award ceremony. During Q2 the leadership team should review the OFIs self-identified during application development and select those that they consider highest priority for the evaluation and improvement cycle that will be completed by KA owners during July.

Q3: KA owners complete a second evaluation and improvement cycle during July, using self-identified OFIs that have been prioritized by leadership as a key input. This results in another update of KA summary documents and a review of KA status by the Category sponsor. These updated KA documents are used to prepare for and host the site visit. Another development opportunity is for select leaders to attend Baldrige Regional Conferences during this time.

Q4: Award programs typically announce recipients and issue feedback reports prior to year-end. The feedback report is reviewed, and then OFIs are numbered and assigned to KA owners. These are key inputs during the January evaluation and improvement cycle. Also during this time leaders should review the assignment of key approaches and update the individual goals of both Category sponsors and KA owners as needed.

The annual cycle described in Table 3.4 provides an efficient, effective, systematic, and integrated approach to design, implement, and refine your operating model for performance excellence. Most organizations find the journey takes 5 to 10 years. Those who persist find it worth the effort.

Develop the Application

Within the annual cycle (Q1–Q2) are key steps related to application development. Figure 3.2 is a swim lane diagram mapping out steps 12–18 and other activities related to application development. This process map assumes that the foundation of key approaches has been established in steps 5–11, as previously described. Steps 12–18 in the diagram are numbered to reference the steps described on the next several pages.

12. *Application Drafts:* The application development team lead has overall responsibility for the following:
    - Develop a timeline of milestones for the application development process and share it with senior leaders, KA owners, Category teams, and key contacts for results.
    - Develop a draft Organizational Profile, based on agreements reached in Steps 2 and / or 6.
    - Develop a table of expected results based on the information included in the Organizational Profile and the results identified during the key approach identification workshops in step 6.

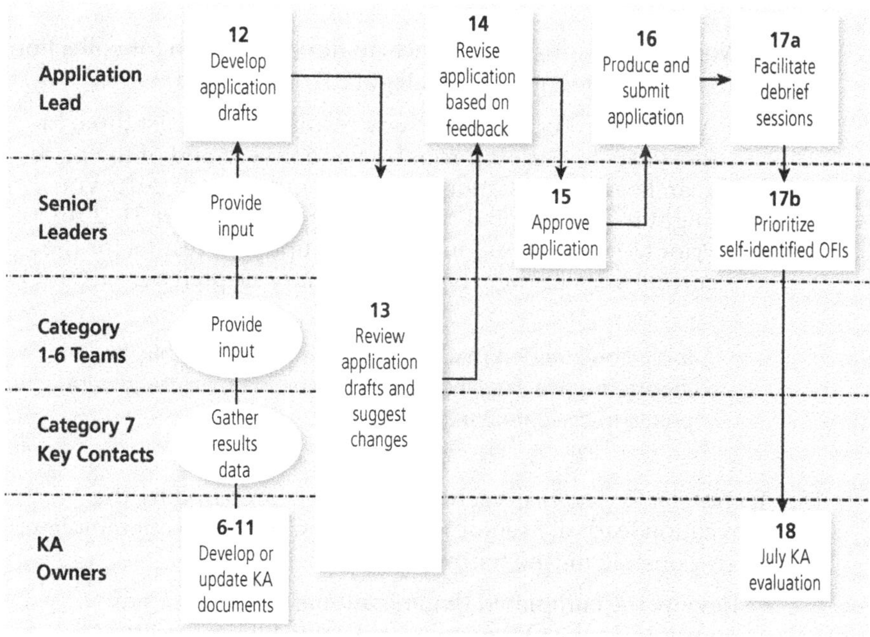

Figure 3.2 Application development process map in swim lane format.

- Develop an outline of key results to include in Category 7. Often this involves clarifying which results will be reported in each area within Category 7 and who will be the source for each one. Refer to Chapter 5 for an explanation of the requirements for Category 7 results.
- Work with KA owners and/or Category teams to prepare a draft of Categories 1–6 by developing additional content (beyond the diagram of key approaches) for each item. This may involve asking Category teams to draft content, or through interviews conducted by the application development team of KA owners and other Category team members to obtain the needed information. In either case, the ultimate result is a draft of the application response for each item in Categories 1–6. The following is a helpful guideline to consider when developing the first draft of an application.

> The response for each item in Categories 1–6 should be approximately three pages in length. Three pages per item multiplied by 12 items in Categories 1–6 equals 36 pages. This leaves 14 pages for reporting of results in Category 7.

- Work with results key contacts to define the plan for collection, display, and reporting of Category 7 results data.
  - Applications typically include results for the past three to five years, reported through calendar year-end of the prior year. For an application submitted in spring of 2016, you might include annual results through December 31, 2015. Prior to site visit you will develop updated results for the current year-to-date, typically January–September or Q1–Q3.

  > It is recommended that at least three years of results be reported, since examiners require a minimum of three data points to evaluate a trend.

13. *Application Reviews:* As each deliverable is prepared by the application lead, the senior leaders and Category team members are responsible for the following:
    - Review the completed Organizational Profile. For any questions in the Organizational Profile where uncertainty remains, the senior leaders schedule time at upcoming meetings or during strategic planning sessions to discuss and determine appropriate responses.

- Review the outline of key results that will be included in the application and the proposed contact for each key result.
- Review drafts of each item in Categories 1–6 and recommend suggested changes.
- Review drafts of each item in Category 7 and recommend suggested changes.

14. *Application Revisions:* The application development team will:
    - Revise the application based on input from senior leaders, KA owners, other Category team members, and results contacts.
    - Finalize the Organizational Profile to align its content with Categories 1–7. This often involves making revisions to the original draft of the Organizational Profile.

> Since the Organizational Profile communicates to examiners the key factors for your organization, it should be the final section revised prior to application submission.

15. *Application Approved:* Senior leaders review and approve the final revision of the application.
16. *Application Production and Submission:* The application development team produces the application, submits it to the award program, and provides copies to all senior leaders, KA owners, process experts, and key contacts for results.
17. *Process Debrief:* The application development team facilitates two different types of debrief sessions:
    (a) With Category sponsors, KA owners, and results key contacts to evaluate and improve the application development process.
    (b) With senior leaders and KA owners to review and prioritize the opportunities identified during the application development process. This review and prioritization:
      - Establishes priorities for the July evaluation and improvement of key approaches, and
      - Allows senior leaders to identify any OFIs that are to be addressed prior to the site visit.

Prepare for and Host Site

18. *July KA Evaluation*: Key approach owners follow the process detailed in Step 26:
    - Review prioritized OFIs from Step 17 during the July evaluation and improvement cycle.
    - Form teams as needed to address opportunities selected for immediate action.
    - Update KA documentation to reflect improvements. Updated KA documents are used to prepare for site visit and to explain key approaches to examiners during the site visit.
19. *Ensure KA Deployment:* Senior leaders and KA owners determine the best way to ensure full deployment of the organization's key approaches with managers, staff, and other key stakeholders such as members of your governance board, key partners, or collaborators. This may involve lunch-and-learn or sharing sessions to review the key approaches. The impetus for this step is the upcoming site visit, but it serves the valuable purpose of more fully deploying key approaches throughout the organization.
20. *Site Visit Preparation:* The application lead works with senior leaders to determine any additional steps that will be taken to prepare the organization for a site visit. This often includes:
    - KA owners develop or update the history of improvement in each key approach document for which they are accountable. What evaluations of the approach have occurred? When did they occur? What facts (data) were used in these evaluations? What opportunities for improvement were identified? What improvements or changes were made in the approach as a result?

      During the site visit, the history of improvement is used to demonstrate that:

      - *Evaluations are systematic:* KA owners should provide the schedule of semi-annual KA review meetings and the agenda for these sessions.
      - *Evaluations are fact-based:* KA owners should describe the data and information reviewed during these sessions.
      - *Improvement is systematic:* KA owners should explain the Check-Act-Plan-Do (CAP-Do) method used to identify and implement improvements. See Step 26 for an example.

Other steps you might consider during site visit preparation include:

- Conduct practice interviews with board members, senior leaders, managers, staff.
- Post updated summaries of key approach documents on the organization's intranet.
- Conduct lunch-and-learn sessions to review key approaches with managers and supervisors.
- Develop a brief "What Everyone Should Know" document and share it with all employees to communicate the key terms and concepts included in the application.
- Administer online quizzes to ensure basic knowledge of key terms and concepts.
- Conduct all-employee meetings to review key terms and concepts and prepare staff.
- Provide talking points for managers to use in preparing their teams for the site visit. Include typical questions that may be asked of any employee during site visit. These are referred to by examiners as "walking around" questions. The following questions are provided for illustration purposes only.

Examples of "walking around" questions that an examiner might ask any employee:

- What are the values of the organization? What is the vision?
- How does your work contribute to the organization's strategic objectives?
- What information do you receive on key organizational results?
- How do you use this information to make decisions?
- What kind of recognition have you personally received?
- When was the last time you attended a formal training class? Topic? Length?
- What knowledge from the training were you able to use back on your job?
- Have you been involved in making improvements in your work? Give examples.
- Are you currently part of any improvement teams?
- What is the team's purpose or goal?
- If you could change one thing about this place, what would it be and why?

You may think that the site visit preparation activities described in Step 20 feel like "studying for the test." While these tactics do help the organization prepare for a more effective site visit, the real benefit is that these activities serve to more fully deploy key approaches and enhance the alignment of staff and key stakeholders with the organization's key factors. The upcoming site visit simply provides a proximate reason for staff to pay attention to this information.

21. *Prepare information for the Examiner Team.* The application lead will:
    - Develop a summary list that identifies the owners for key approaches, and the key contacts for results, and share this with the examiner team when requested.
    - Work with key contacts for results to develop updated year-to-date results for all of Category 7.
    - Work with the examiner team to finalize logistics including hotel, meeting rooms, and so on.
    - Develop an opening presentation to share with the examiner team during the site visit kick-off meeting with senior leaders.
22. *Host Site Visit.* During the site visit:
    - The application lead works closely with the lead examiner to coordinate examiner interviews, address questions or issues, and ensure a successful visit.
    - Managers and staff use KA summaries as an aid when responding to examiner questions.
    - The organization uses the site visit as an opportunity for learning. The questions asked by examiners can help leaders reflect on current approaches and identify opportunities to improve.
23. *Debrief Site Visit:* At the conclusion of the site visit, the application lead facilitates a debrief session with senior leaders, KA owners, and Category team members to:
    - Evaluate and improve the approaches used to prepare for and host the site visit.
    - Identify the OFIs that are likely to be included in the feedback report, based on the learning and opportunities identified through discussion with the examiners. Add these to the OFI log for review in Step 24.

Use the Feedback

24. *Analyze Feedback Report:* The application lead receives the feedback report from the award office, reviews the document, and prepares to share the feedback with senior leaders. Steps taken include:

    - Number each Opportunity for Improvement (OFI) in the feedback report (e.g., from 1–50) for ease of reference.
    - Identify whether each OFI is related to basic, overall, or multiple (BOM) level requirements.
    - Assign each OFI received in Categories 1–6 to the most appropriate key approach.
    - Also assign any self-identified OFIs that were logged by the organization during application development or site visit debrief, even if not included in the feedback report.
    - Review Strength comments to identify any instances where further refinement of the related approach could create a significant advantage for the organization.
    - Review Category 7 Results OFIs. These are generally of two types:
        - *Poor performance* involves results OFIs where the current level or trend is not favorable relative to an appropriate comparison. In this case, one of the key approaches in Categories 1–6 will need to be improved in order to produce a better result for this key performance measure.
        - *Missing information* involves results OFIs where no results are reported, or comparisons or segmentation are not provided for an important result. In this case one of the key approaches for measurement should be modified to provide the necessary information.

    In other words, the best response is usually to assign results OFIs to the owner of the most appropriate key approach. In theory, all results OFIs for missing information could be assigned to the Scorecard Development Process (Item 4.1a), which is used to select key performance indicators and comparisons. However, in many cases results OFIs are more appropriately assigned to the key process in Categories 1–6 that is most directly related to the result. These relationships are summarized in Table 3.5.

Table 3.5 Alignment of results OFIs with approaches in Categories 1–6.

Result OFIs	Assign to the owner of the related key approach
7.1a	6.1a(1) Measures of key product and process requirements 6.1b(3) Measures of the performance/improvement of key work processes
7.1b(1)	6.1b(1) In-process measures for key work processes 6.1b(2) Measures of key support processes
7.1b(2)	6.2c(2) Measures of emergency preparedness
7.1c	6.2b Measures of supply chain management
7.2a(1)	3.1b(1) Measures of customer satisfaction and dissatisfaction 3.2b(2) Measures of complaint management 3.1b(2) Measures of customer satisfaction relative to competitors, other organizations offering similar products/services, or benchmarks
7.2a(2)	3.1b(1) Measures of customer engagement 3.2b(1) Measures of customer relationship building over the customer life cycle
7.3a(1)	5.1a Measures of workforce capability and capacity 2.2a(4) Measures of key workforce plans
7.3a(2)	Measures of workforce climate including: 5.1b(1) Workforce health and security 6.2c(1) Workforce safety 5.1b(2) Workforce services and benefits
7.3a(3)	5.2a Measures of workforce engagement and satisfaction
7.3a(4)	5.2b Measures of workforce and leader development
7.4a(1)	1.1a/b Measures of senior leaders communication and engagement with the workforce and key customers to deploy vision and values, encourage two-way communication and create a focus on action
7.4a(2)	1.2a Measures of governance and fiscal accountability
7.4a(3)	1.2b(1) Measures of meeting and surpassing regulatory and legal requirements
7.4a(4)	1.2b(2) Measures of ethical behavior and of stakeholder trust in your senior leaders and governance, and measures of breaches of ethical behavior
7.4a(5)	1.2c(1) Measures of fulfillment of your societal responsibilities 1.2c(2) Measures of support of your key communities

(Continued)

Table 3.5 Alignment of results OFIs with approaches in Categories 1–6 *(continued).*

Result OFIs	Assign to the owner of the related key approach	
7.4b	2.1b	Measures of achievement of organizational strategy (strategic objectives)
	2.2a(5)	Measures of achievement of your organization's action plans
	2.1a(2) and 6.1c	Measures for innovation and taking intelligent risks
	2.1a(4)	Measures for building and strengthening core competencies
7.5a(1)	4.1a	Measures of financial performance
7.5a(2)	3.2a(3)	Measures of marketplace performance (for each key customer group or market segment)

NOTE: Chapter 5 describes the recommended approach to align strategic planning (2.1) with organizational scorecards (4.1) and key results (Category 7).

25. *Senior Leader Review of Feedback Report and OFI Assignments:* Senior leaders review the assignment of OFIs to owners of key approaches or results. Senior leaders should also review the entire feedback report to:

   - Identify any key OFIs that require cross-functional efforts and/or cannot be addressed effectively by a single key approach owner. Often these are identified in the Executive Summary of the feedback report as cross-cutting issues. As an example, it is common early in the journey for organizations to receive an OFI related to the alignment of strategic objectives and goals (Category 2) with key performance measures (Category 4) and key results (Category 7). This may require involvement of the entire senior leadership team and would typically be resolved through the Strategic Planning Process.
   - Identify two to three key approaches and related OFIs that have the greatest strategic importance to the organization based on mission, vision and/or strategic objectives in order to ensure these OFIs are addressed appropriately. Often this will involve establishing stretch goals for innovation (discontinuous or breakthrough improvement) of the key approach because of its strategic importance. Recall from Chapter 2 that your aim should be to achieve the 50–65% scoring band for all key approaches and the 70–85% scoring band for a few key approaches of strategic importance. To fully address all the requirements of the 50–65% scoring band and move into the 70–85% band requires that a fact-based, systematic evaluation and improvement process and some organizational learning, including innovation, are in place for improving the efficiency and effectiveness of key processes. (L)

Improve Key Approaches

26. *January KA Evaluation:* KA owners complete the evaluation and improvement during January in similar fashion to the July process that was described in Step 18. The key difference in January is that KA owners treat the OFIs that were assigned to their key approach in Steps 24–25 as one of the key inputs to inform the January evaluation and improvement cycle. As before, KA owners can form improvement teams as needed to address OFIs and must ensure that KA documentation is updated based on any changes made. These updated KAs are used to develop the next application beginning in February. Refer to Steps 30–33.

    The KA evaluations conducted in January and July must be systematic and fact-based in order to achieve the top end of the 50–65% scoring band. If your organization has a well-defined continuous improvement method, this may be appropriate for KA reviews. The approach defined for your 4.1b/c Scorecard Review process or 6.1b Process Improvement process may also provide an effective process for KA evaluation and improvement meetings.

    Regardless of the method or process used, to ensure that evaluation and improvement sessions are systematic and fact-based, KA evaluation sessions should be:

    - Scheduled in advance (e.g., January and July),
    - Follow a well-defined and common agenda, and
    - Use appropriate data to inform the evaluation.

    The approach used for KA evaluation is often modeled after the CAP-Do process shown in Figure 3.1. Following is an example of a KA evaluation and improvement method. It includes references to each stage in the CAP-Do cycle.

    Example of a Systematic, Fact-based KA Evaluation and Improvement Process (CAP-Do)

    Check

    Before the KA Meeting:

    (1) Schedule KA evaluation/improvement meeting (two per year, e.g., January and July)

    (2) KA owners or their assigned delegates gather needed data/information/feedback. This includes identification of possible opportunities for improvement (OFIs) from at least four different sources.

- **OFIs based on review of performance data** for measures of the key approach. Recall that in Step 11, KA owners were asked to identify the key performance measures that provide a meaningful evaluation of the effectiveness and efficiency of each key approach.
- **OFIs from award program feedback reports.** Feedback reports are typically received in December and OFIs assigned to the appropriate KA owner as described in Step 24. During the January meeting, these OFIs from the feedback report are key inputs to the KA evaluation.
- **Self-identified OFIs** are a key input for KA evaluation in both January and July. Any OFIs that have been self-identified since the last KA evaluation meeting should be recorded in the OFI log as described in Steps 9 and 24 and considered a key input.
  - For the July KA evaluation, most of these OFIs will have been self-identified as a result of application development (Steps 12–18).
  - For the January KA evaluation, most will have been identified as a result of the site visit and debrief (Steps 22–23).
  - For both July and January evaluations, OFIs may have been self-identified as a result of key approach observations performed by the KA owner and/or his delegate(s). After any change in a key approach is made, it is recommended that observations be performed to monitor implementation and ensure full deployment of the change. An additional benefit of KA observations is that they provide the opportunity to obtain direct feedback from employees who operate the process. This input will often identify additional opportunities for improvement in the key approach.
- **OFIs resulting from new requirements** when Criteria are revised in January every other year.
  - In years when the Criteria are revised, the KA owner and his/her team should review the changes in the Criteria during the January evaluation session to understand new or modified requirements and identify key OFIs relative to these new requirements. Each addition to the Criteria requirements represents a possible OFI.

Act

During the KA meeting:

(3) Review the requirements of the Criteria that are addressed by this key approach.

(4) Assess how well the key approach meets these requirements. This assessment should consider all sources of OFIs as described in the Check step of CAP-Do.

(5) Review the "History of Improvement" in order to follow up on the status of any improvements planned during the last evaluation and improvement cycle. Have they been implemented? Were they effective? If not, they remain OFIs and should be included in the prioritization in the next step.

(6) Determine priorities for improvement. In some cases, multiple OFIs will be identified and the KA owner will need to prioritize which ones will be addressed during the coming months.

Is it necessary to address every OFI?

KA owners should review all identified OFIs, but are not required to address each one. In general, you should address all OFIs that refer to ADLI at the basic or overall level, but may choose not to address some OFIs for multiple level approaches or deployment of approaches to some units or groups unless there is a clear benefit for doing so.

Must address OFIs for:	May choose not to address OFIs for:
• Basic or overall approaches that are not fully systematic (A) • Approaches that lack fact-based, systematic evaluation and improvement (L) • Approaches not fully integrated with organizational needs or other key processes (I)	• Approaches that do not address multiple requirements (A) if KA owner determines these are not critical to organizational success or sustainability • Lack of deployment (D) of approaches to areas that are deemed of little importance to organizational success or sustainability

Plan

(7) Develop an action plan to improve the key approach:

- Specify *What* actions will be completed, *Who* is responsible for each step, and *When* each action step is expected to be complete. Action plans to improve a key approach will often include actions to:
  - Benchmark the best practices of Baldrige award recipients for the key approach, as appropriate.
  - Update the key approach documentation.
  - Communicate and train staff in changes to the approach. In some cases this may involve updates of the standard work or procedures for the process.
  - Collect data, observe the process, or obtain feedback to determine whether the improvement has been effective.
  - Report progress to the KA owner and / or sponsor during and after implementation of the planned improvements.

Do

After the KA meeting:

(8) Update the KA document to reflect any changes to be implemented in the key approach. Record the results of the evaluation / improvement cycle in the history of improvement.

(9) Follow the action plan developed in Step 7 to implement changes in the key approach. Changes should not be considered fully implemented until they are:

- Communicated and trained, so that staff or other key stakeholders are aware of changes and able to perform the new or modified process.
- Observed, to ensure they have been deployed and can be sustained. Observation of the actual process is a key method to ensure changes have been effectively deployed and can be sustained over time. It provides an opportunity to coach and provide feedback to those performing the process, and also to gather input from employees that can be used to identify additional opportunities for improvement in the key approach.

(10) Report progress and results to the KA owner during/after implementation and repeat CAP-Do:

- *Check* – Use observations and any other methods or measures identified in the action plan to review whether the change is on track, fully deployed, effective, and sustained.
- *Act* – Based on the results of these reviews, determine what additional actions are needed.
- *Plan* – Develop an action plan.
- *Do* – Implement the plan.
- *Repeat* CAP-Do until improvements in the key approach are fully deployed.

27. *Category Sponsors Review KA Status:* After the January KA evaluation meetings are complete, Category sponsors should meet with each of their KA owners to:
    - Ensure that all OFIs assigned to the KA owner have been considered and addressed appropriately.
    - Understand the rationale for any decisions by KA owners not to address OFIs for multiple level approach requirements.
    - Review the improvement plans for each key approach and ensure the identified actions are sufficient to address the OFI.
    - Ensure appropriate resources are available to support KA improvement plans.
    - Identify areas where coordination with KA owners in other Category teams may be needed.
    - Ensure appropriate actions are identified to follow-up and determine whether changes in the key approach have been implemented and are effective.
    - Ensure that KA documentation has been updated.

The update of KA documentation in January leads directly into the development of the next application beginning in February.

Develop Future Applications

Future applications are developed using a simplified version of the process previously described.

28. The Application Development Team lead develops a timeline with deadlines for key inputs, including updates of key approach documentation by KA owners and updates of key results data by contacts for key results.

29. Application Development Kick-off Meeting: Prior to the beginning of application development in February, the Application Development Team should conduct a meeting with the Leadership Team, all Category Sponsors, and KA owners. This meeting is used to:
    - Review the timeline for application development, including deadlines for updates of key approach documentation, updates of key results data, and the schedule of interviews with KA owners to gather input for application development.
    - Review a high-level summary of improvements being implemented in key approaches.
    - Ensure appropriate resources are available to support KA improvement plans. Where one or more individuals are required to address several KA plans, agree on the timing for use of these resources.
    - As follow-up to Step 25, discuss and agree on the approach that will be used to address any key OFIs that require cross-functional efforts and/or cannot be addressed effectively by a single key approach owner.
    - As follow-up to Step 25, ensure that two to three key OFIs with the greatest strategic importance to the organization based on mission, vision and/or strategic objectives are being appropriately addressed. This often involves setting stretch goals for innovation in these key approaches.
    - Ensure that all other OFIs from the feedback report are being appropriately addressed.
    - Understand the rationale for any decisions by KA owners not to address OFIs for multiple level approach requirements.
30. KA owners and result key contacts provide updated information prior to the deadline.
31. The application lead works with:
    - KA owners to understand changes in key approaches.
    - The application team to update the application and reflect changes in Categories 1–6.
    - Results contacts to update Category 7 results based on the information provided.
    - Senior leaders to update the Organizational Profile.
32. Senior leaders review and approve the entire application.
33. Submit the application and prepare for the site visit.

34. Receive and use the feedback as described in Steps 24–28 to improve key approaches.
35. Repeat until the organization achieves performance excellence and / or becomes Baldrige-worthy.

If you think this sounds like a lot of work, you are correct. Who said excellence would be easy?

SUMMARY OF THE ROAD MAP

The steps described in this chapter provide a well-defined method for using the Criteria to build an integrated performance excellence system. This method uses:

- Key approaches for the 28 areas to address in Category 1–6 as the foundation of the performance excellence system, and
- Feedback from self-assessment and award programs as a means to evaluate and improve these key approaches over time.

It should be clear that while significant effort is required to build the first application, the documentation of key approaches streamlines the process of developing future applications significantly. They are also the means of documenting the organization's history of improvement and they enable effective use of feedback reports to evaluate and improve these key approaches. Finally, they simplify site visit, by providing managers with aids to use when responding to examiner questions.

It generally takes at least three application cycles (with genuine improvement in your key approaches between each submission) for organizations to achieve a score of 65%. If you apply annually, this would require three years. If you apply every other year, six years would likely be needed, though it can be done sooner if significant progress is made between application submissions.

Since the semi-annual KA reviews using self-assessment and award program feedback provide fact-based evaluation of key approaches, at least three cycles are generally required to provide a meaningful history of improvement for each approach, with innovation evident in some areas of strategic importance.

In addition, three results data points are required as evidence of improvement trends for Category 7 results. Many organizations find they do not measure some key results that are required by the Criteria until they begin the journey. This is another reason it often takes a minimum of three years to implement a fully integrated Baldrige-based performance excellence system. It is possible to accomplish this more quickly if your organization has already achieved role model (i.e., top decile, industry leading, or benchmark) performance results across the key result areas within Category 7 before you begin using the Criteria.

The next chapter provides a summary of the key approaches that are recommended to meet overall requirements for the 28 areas to address within Categories 1–6. They provide the typical starting point for design and deployment of a performance excellence system.

4
Recommended Key Approaches for Categories 1–6

The design of an organization's operating model for performance excellence often begins with the 35 key approaches summarized in this chapter. They are the recommended starting point for responding to the overall requirements of the 28 areas to address in Categories 1–6. Once established, these key approaches become the focal point of award applications and the object of semi-annual evaluation and improvement cycles as described in Chapter 3.

The approaches recommended here align with the typical practices and needs of most organizations. However, a first self-assessment relative to the Criteria will usually lead most organizations to conclude that either more or fewer than the 35 key approaches shown are required for their operating model. The recommended key approaches will be combined or separated, based on the current methods used by the organization and the need to assign accountability for each key approach to an appropriate owner. By beginning with the 35 key approaches summarized in Tables 4.1 to 4.6 an organization can minimize the number of wrong turns taken when defining its own operating model in year one of the journey.

The information in these tables is organized around the 28 areas to address within Categories 1–6 of the Criteria. Each table includes three columns:

- The area to address (e.g., 1.1a Vision, Values, and Mission).
- The recommended key approach (in bold) for each area to address, with a brief description of the processes it includes and references to other aligned key approaches. The names given to these key approaches are for descriptive purposes only. Each organization will use its own terminology when naming key approaches.
- The overall requirements met by this recommended key approach.

Note that in most cases, one key approach is recommended for each area to address. For several areas, more than one key approach is used to respond separately to the multiple requirements. For example, for 3.2b Customer Relationships, two key approaches are recommended:

- Customer Relationship Management [3.2b(1)] and
- Complaint Management [3.2b(2)].

In several instances, an approach for one area is used to address the requirements in another area. These references are included in the table. For example, the 5.1a Workforce Planning Process is recommended as the approach to meet the requirement for development of workforce plans in 2.2a(4).

The business/nonprofit Criteria are used in the tables that follow. There are some minor differences in the Criteria for Education and Health Care, primarily in Item 6.1.

LEADERSHIP

Table 4.1 Summary of key approaches recommended to meet overall requirements of Category 1.

Area to address	Recommended key approach	Overall requirements
1.1a Vision, Values, and Mission	**Leadership System** Includes the multiple processes, methods, and/or behaviors required of leaders to deploy mission, vision and values, listen to customers, set goals, plan and align resources, develop and motivate staff, manage and improve performance, and innovate for the future. This approach is often established in year two of the journey to clarify expectations for leaders to execute the key processes in Categories 1–6 that comprise the organization's operating model for performance excellence. In the first year of the journey, you may address these overall requirements via senior leaders' active participation in the following key approaches: 1.1a(1) Vision and Values – Leaders set/review vision and values, often as part of 2.1a Strategy Development process 1.1a(2) Promote Legal and Ethical Behavior – Leaders actively participate in 1.2b Compliance Program	1.1a(1) Vision and Values **How do senior leaders set your organization's vision and values?** 1.1a(2) Promoting Legal and Ethical Behavior **How do senior leaders' actions demonstrate their commitment to legal and ethical behavior?** 1.1a(3) Creating a Successful Organization **How do senior leaders' actions build an organization that is successful now and in the future?**

(Continued)

Table 4.1 Summary of key approaches recommended to meet overall requirements of Category 1 *(continued)*.

Area to address	Recommended key approach	Overall requirements
1.1a Vision, Values, and Mission *(continued)*	1.1a(3) Creating a Successful Organization – Leaders actively participate in other processes such as: 2.1a Strategic Planning 2.2a Action Planning 4.1b/c Scorecard Analysis, Review, and Organizational Improvement Process 3.2a Product or Service Innovation Process 6.1b Process Management 6.1c Innovation Management	
1.1b Communication and organizational performance	**Senior Leader Communication Process** Includes multiple methods used by senior leaders to communicate with the workforce and key customers. This approach aligns with: • Leadership System (1.1a) • Voice of Customer (3.1a) • Customer Relationship Management (3.2b) • Action Planning (2.2a) • Scorecard Review and Organizational Improvement (4.1b/c) • Workforce Performance Management (5.2a)	1.1b(1) Communication **How do senior leaders communicate with and engage the entire workforce and key customers?** 1.1b(2) Focus on Action **How do senior leaders create a focus on action that will achieve the organization's mission?**
1.2a Organizational governance	**Governance and Leadership Improvement** Includes policies, processes, and methods used to manage interactions with the governing board, including audits (1.2b) and reviews of senior leader performance [5.2a(4)]. Also includes participation by the Board and senior leaders in succession planning and leadership development processes (5.2b).	1.2a(1) Governance System **How does your organization ensure responsible governance?** 1.2a(2) Performance Evaluation **How do you evaluate the performance of your senior leaders, including the chief executive, and your governance board?**

(Continued)

Table 4.1 Summary of key approaches recommended to meet overall requirements of Category 1 *(continued)*.

Area to address	Recommended key approach	Overall requirements
1.2b Legal and ethical behavior	**Compliance Program** Processes and measures used to manage risk and ensure legal, ethical, and regulatory compliance. Refer to the GLERCAP scorecard in Chapter 5 for a summary of the recommended process to address: • **G**overnance • **L**egal • **E**thical • **R**egulatory Compliance • **A**ccreditation, and • Emergency **P**reparedness	1.2b(1) Legal and Regulatory Compliance **How do you anticipate and address public concerns with your products and operations?** 1.2b(2) Ethical Behavior **How do you promote and ensure ethical behavior in all interactions?**
1.2c Societal responsibilities	**Societal Responsibility and Community Support** Process to assess the organization's impact on society and its key communities, determine areas for involvement, and take actions to support and strengthen them. In health care the CHNA (Community Health Needs Assessment) is often the key process used to address this requirement. Depending on how an organization views its relationship with the community, some organizations may integrate this approach with one of two other processes: • Customer Relationship Management process (3.2b) or • GLERCAP scorecard used to manage risks (1.2b)	1.2c(1) Societal Well-Being **How do you consider societal well-being and benefit as part of strategy and daily operations?** 1.2c(2) Community Support **How do you actively support and strengthen your key communities?**

STRATEGY

Table 4.2 Summary of key approaches recommended to meet overall requirements of Category 2.

Area to address	Recommended key approach	Overall requirements
2.1a Strategy Development Process	**Strategic Planning Process** Process to assess the organization's environment and competitive situation and develop strategies and objectives to respond to key challenges and advantages. This approach is often operated annually to update or develop: • Strategies (2.1a) and Strategic Objectives (2.1b) • Scorecards (4.1a) • Projections [2.2a(6)] and Goals (2.1b) • Action Plans (2.2a) Strategic Planning either includes or closely aligns with: • Work System Evaluation Process [2.1a(4)] • Projection and Goal Setting Process [2.2a(6), 4.1c(2)] • Budgeting Process [2.2a(3)]. Refer to 2.2a Action Planning for more on Budgeting.	2.1a(1) Strategic Planning Process **How do you conduct strategic planning?** 2.1a(2) Innovation **How does your strategy development process stimulate and incorporate innovation?** 2.1a(3) Strategy Considerations **How do you collect and analyze relevant data and develop information for your strategic planning process?**
	Work System Evaluation Process [2.1a(4)] Could be part of Strategic Planning or separate; this process is used to: • Determine key work systems • Assess key work systems relative to core competencies • Determine how best to configure internal and external resources to support strategy • Make decisions to determine what work is outsourced to key suppliers/partners (6.2b) and what work will comprise the organization's key work processes [6.1a(1)]	2.1a(4) Work Systems and Core Competencies **What are your key work systems?**

(Continued)

Table 4.2 Summary of key approaches recommended to meet overall requirements of Category 2 *(continued)*.

Area to address	Recommended key approach	Overall requirements
2.1a Strategy Development Process *(continued)*	**Projection and Goal Setting Process [2.2a(6), 4.1c(2)]** Process to develop projections and evaluate comparisons in order to establish short- and longer-term goals for strategic objectives. Goals set using this process are: • Included in 2.1a Strategic Planning Process • Used to initiate 2.2a Action Planning • Aligned with 4.1a Scorecard Development/Update Process used to select key measures and comparisons • Used to evaluate progress in 4.1b/c Scorecard Analysis, Review and Organizational Improvement Process • Aligned with 5.2a Performance Management Process	4.1c(2) Future Performance **How do you project your organization's future performance?** 2.2a(6) Performance Projections **For the key performance measures or indicators [in 2.2a(5)], what are your performance projections for short- and longer-term planning horizons?**
2.1b Strategic Objectives	**Strategic Plan Objectives** This summary of the organization's strategic plan includes: • Strategic objectives • Key measures of success • Projections and comparisons • Key goals and timetables for accomplishment of strategic objectives (both short- and longer-term) • Key strategies to respond to challenges, leverage advantages, and pursue opportunities	2.1b(1) Key Strategic Objectives **What are your organization's key strategic objectives and timetable for achieving them?** 2.1b(2) Strategic Objective Considerations **How do your strategic objectives achieve appropriate balance among varying and potentially competing organizational needs?**

(Continued)

Table 4.2 Summary of key approaches recommended to meet overall requirements of Category 2 *(continued)*.

Area to address	Recommended key approach	Overall requirements
2.2a Action Plan Development and Deployment	**Action Planning Process** Action planning can operate as a stand-alone process and as a continuation of the Projection and Goal Setting Process [2.2a(6), 4.1c(2)]. It includes methods used for: • Development of action plans to achieve strategic objectives and key goals • Deployment of action plans and key goals • Budgeting [(2.2a(3)] to ensure appropriate allocation of resources to achieve strategic objectives (2.1b) This process is aligned with other key approaches such as: • Budgeting process [2.2a(3)] • Scorecard Analysis, Review and Organizational Improvement Process [4.1b/c], which is used to review progress toward accomplishment of action plans (2.2a) and often results in the modification of action plans (2.2b).	2.2a(1) Action Plans **What are key short- and longer-term action plans?** 2.2a(2) Action Plan Implementation **How do you deploy action plans?**
	Budgeting Process [2.2a(3)] Resource allocation is typically accomplished through the Budgeting process. This can operate as a stand-alone process or as a sub-process within Action Planning (2.2a). This approach is also aligned with the Workforce Planning Process [5.1a(1), 2.2a(4)] as staffing plans are key components of the budget for most organizations.	2.2a(3) Resource Allocation **How do you ensure that financial and other resources are available to support the achievement of action plans while you meet current obligations?**

(Continued)

Table 4.2 Summary of key approaches recommended to meet overall requirements of Category 2 *(continued)*.

Area to address	Recommended key approach	Overall requirements
2.2a Action Plan Development and Deployment *(continued)*	**Workforce Planning Process [5.1a(1), 2.2a(4)]** This process is a specific application of the 2.2a Action Planning Process for development of workforce plans to support achievement of strategic objectives and key goals. Workforce Planning [5.1a] is the process used to develop Workforce Plans [2.2a(4)]. It includes an assessment of the organization's capacity and capability needs to determine the workforce plans needed to support achievement of strategic objectives, key goals, and other action plans to implement changes in products and services, customers and markets, suppliers and partners, and operations [2.1a].	2.2a(4) Workforce Plans **What are key workforce plans to support short- and longer-term strategic objectives and action plans?**
	4.1a Scorecard Development/ Update Process is the process used to determine the key performance measures [2.2a(5)] that will be used to track daily operations and overall organizational performance [4.1a(1)]. Key performance measures: • Are summarized in the Strategic Plan (2.1b) • Are aligned with Action Plans (2.2a) and Scorecards (4.1a) • May also include measures associated with Customer Satisfaction Measurement (3.1b), Product or Service Innovation (3.2a), Workforce Planning (5.1a), Workforce Engagement [5.2a(2-3)], Workforce Performance Management [5.2a(1,4)], Process Design and Improvement (6.1a/b), Innovation Management (6.1c), Cost Control (6.2a), Supply Chain Management (6.2b), etc. • Are the key input to the Scorecard Analysis, Review and Organizational Improvement Process [4.1b/c]	2.2a(5) Performance Measures **What key performance measures or indicators do you use to track the achievement and effectiveness of your action plans?**

(Continued)

Table 4.2 Summary of key approaches recommended to meet overall requirements of Category 2 *(continued)*.

Area to address	Recommended key approach	Overall requirements
2.2b Action Plan Modification	The **2.2a Action Planning Process** described previously is also used to modify or update action plans as needed. This is often triggered by findings from processes such as: • Scorecard Analysis, Review, and Organizational Improvement Process [4.1b/c] • Customer Satisfaction Measurement (3.1b) • Workforce Performance Management [5.2a(1,4)] • Process Design and Improvement (6.1a/b) • Supply Chain Management (6.2b)	2.2b Action Plan Modification **How do you establish and implement modified action plans if circumstances require a shift in plans & rapid execution of new plans?**

CUSTOMERS

Table 4.3 Summary of key approaches recommended to meet overall requirements of Category 3.

Area to address	Recommended key approach	Overall requirements
3.1a Customer listening	**Voice of the Customer (VOC) Process** Includes the multiple methods used to listen to customers in order to understand their preferences, expectations, and requirements. This process aligns with: • Senior leader communication with key customers (1.1b) • Customer satisfaction measurement (3.1b) • Product or Service Innovation (3.2a) • Customer/Market segmentation [3.2a(3)] • Customer relationship building (3.2b)	3.1a(1) Current Customers **How do you listen to, interact with, and observe customers to obtain actionable information?** 3.1a(2) Potential Customers **How do you listen to potential customers to obtain actionable information?**

(Continued)

Table 4.3 Summary of key approaches recommended to meet overall requirements of Category 3 *(continued).*

Area to address	Recommended key approach	Overall requirements
3.1b Determination of customer satisfaction and engagement	**Customer Satisfaction Measurement (CSM)** Typically includes the methods used for administration of surveys to measure customer satisfaction, dissatisfaction, and engagement. This approach is also used as an input for: • Review of customer data [4.1a(3)] • Segmentation of customers [3.2a(3)] • Complaint management [3.2b(2)]	3.1b(1) Satisfaction, Dissatisfaction, and Engagement **How do you determine customer satisfaction, dissatisfaction, and engagement?** 3.1b(2) Satisfaction Relative to Competitors **How do you obtain information on customers' satisfaction with your organization relative to other organizations?**
3.2a Product/ Service Offerings and Customer Support	**Product or Service Innovation Process (PSIP)** Process used to identify new or modified offerings. This process may involve a combination of market or product planning and new product development. This approach can also be used to meet requirements in 6.1a for design of products/services/programs. This approach aligns with: • 3.1a VOC process and 3.1b Customer Satisfaction Measurement to determine key requirements, and • 6.1a/b Process Design and Improvement process to implement new offerings.	3.2a(1) Product/Service Offerings **How do you determine product offerings?** 6.1a(1) Product/Service Requirements **How do you determine key product requirements?** 6.1a(2) Design Concepts **How do you design your products to meet requirements?**
	Customer Segmentation is enabled by the **Customer Satisfaction Measurement (3.1b) process**. It is typically accomplished through one of two processes: • 3.2a Product or Service Innovation Process or • 3.2b Customer Relationship Management Process	3.2a(3) Customer Segmentation **How do you determine your customer groups and market segments?**

(Continued)

Table 4.3 Summary of key approaches recommended to meet overall requirements of Category 3 *(continued).*

Area to address	Recommended key approach	Overall requirements
3.2b Customer Relationships	**Customer Relationship Management and Support Processes [3.2b(1), 3.2a(2)]** The multiple methods used to support customers and build relationships at each stage of the customer life cycle. Includes methods to: • Acquire new customers [via processes for Marketing, Sales, etc.] • Satisfy and retain existing customers [via customer support in 3.2a(2) and/ or service delivery in 6.1b] • Enhance customer engagement [via product/service offerings in 3.2a or customer relationship building in 3.2b]	3.2b(1) Relationship Management **How do you build and manage customer relationships?** 3.2a(2) Customer Support **How do you enable customers to seek information and support?**
	Complaint Management Process [3.2b(2)] The process to respond and recover when customers complain. The service recovery component of complaint management must be integrated with the approaches used to build customer relationships in order to enhance engagement (3.2b). Complaint management data can serve as a key input to processes such as: • Product or Service Innovation (3.2a) • Workforce Performance Management (5.2a) • Learning & Development (5.2b) or • Process Design and Improvement (6.1a)	3.2b(2) Complaint Management **How do you manage customer complaints?**

MEASUREMENT, ANALYSIS, KNOWLEDGE MANAGEMENT

Table 4.4 Summary of key approaches recommended to meet overall requirements of Category 4.

Area to address	Recommended key approach	Overall requirements
Social Media Strategy Though not a specific area to address, many organizations will find it helpful to define a process that is used to develop and implement their social media strategy. Depending on the target audiences and objectives of this process, it can be used to address the multiple requirements in several other areas: • 1.1b Senior leader communication with the workforce and key customers • 3.1a Voice of customer listening • 3.2b Customer relationship management • Workforce processes (e.g., 5.1a hiring, 5.1b benefits management, 5.2a engagement, 5.2b learning and development) • 6.2b Supply chain management		**Social Media Strategy** To master the opportunities and challenges of social media and web-based technologies in order to support and enhance senior leader communication, customer listening, hiring, training, management and engagement of the workforce, and supply chain management.
4.1a Performance Measurement	**Scorecard Development/Update Process** To select key performance measures and comparisons and collect/report the data included on organizational scorecards at all levels and in all parts of the organization. Scorecards are used to: • Deploy objectives and goals (2.1b) • Track achievement of action plans (2.2a) • Review, analyze, and improve organizational performance (4.1b/c) • Control and improve key work processes (6.1b) • Control costs (6.2a) • Manage key suppliers (6.2b) • Manage innovation (6.1c) • Manage product or service offerings (3.2a) • Improve customer satisfaction (3.1b) • Improve customer relationships (3.2b)	4.1a(1) Performance Measures **How do you use data and information to track daily operations and overall organizational performance?** 2.2a(5) Performance Measures **What key performance measures do you use to track the achievement and effectiveness of your action plans?** 4.1a(2) Comparative Data **How do you select and effectively use comparative data & info?** 4.1a(3) Customer Data **How do you use VOC and market data/ info?**

(Continued)

Table 4.4 Summary of key approaches recommended to meet overall requirements of Category 4 *(continued).*

Area to address	Recommended key approach	Overall requirements
4.1a Performance Measurement *(continued)*	**Scorecard Development/Update Process** • Improve the workforce environment (5.1a/b) • Improve workforce engagement [5.2a(1-3)] • Improve workforce performance [5.2a(4)] • Monitor compliance (GLERCAP, 1.2a, 6.2c) This process is enabled by approaches to ensure quality and availability of data (4.2b). This process is improved through evaluations to ensure measurement agility [4.1a(4)].	4.1a(4) Measurement Agility **How do you ensure that your performance measurement system can respond to rapid or unexpected organizational or external changes?**
4.1b Performance Analysis and Review	**Scorecard Analysis, Review, and Organizational Improvement Process [4.1b/c]*** This process is a common element within an integrated system for review of scorecards and performance data at all levels and in all parts of the organization. The common review process is used to assess performance, identify opportunities, and take the appropriate actions to improve. Reviews are typically based on the scorecards established in 4.1a and follow a CAP-Do process (Figure 3.1) to: • Collect/report key results (scorecards) • Analyze data to understand causes of poor performance • Analyze data to identify high performing units and best practices • Develop projections to identify gaps • Determine review findings and priorities • Deploy priorities for improvement and opportunities for innovation	4.1b Performance Analysis and Review **How do review your organization's performance and capabilities?** *Other related requirements* 4.1a(3) Customer Data **How do you use voice of customer and market data/info?** 5.2a(3) Assessment of Engagement **How do you assess workforce engagement?** 6.1b(3) Product and Process Improvement **How do improve your work processes to improve products and performance, enhance core competencies, reduce variability?**

(Continued)

Table 4.4 Summary of key approaches recommended to meet overall requirements of Category 4 *(continued)*.

Area to address	Recommended key approach	Overall requirements
4.1b Performance Analysis and Review *(continued)*	**Scorecard Analysis, Review, and Organizational Improvement Process [4.1b/c]*** • Take the appropriate action to continually improve, which could initiate any of the following processes: – Goal setting [2.2a(6), 4.1c(2)] – Action planning (2.2a) – Action plan updates (2.2b) – Product or Service Innovation (3.2a) – Customer relationship management (3.2b) – Share best practices (4.1c) – Manage organizational knowledge (4.2a) – Develop/update workforce plans (5.1a) – Coach or train staff (5.2a/b) – Improve key work processes (6.1b) – Control costs (6.2a) – Work with key suppliers (6.2b) * *The organization's own version of the CAP-Do process can be deployed as a common approach to continuous improvement that is integrated within nearly all the processes identified here.*	
4.1c Performance Improvement	The **4.1b/c Scorecard Analysis, Review, and Organizational Improvement Process** described previously can be used to identify and implement improvements in almost any area: • Achievement of strategic objectives and goals (2.1b) • Accomplishment of action plans (2.2a) • Key work processes (6.1b) • Cost control (6.2a) • Supplier performance (6.2b) • Innovation (6.1c)	4.1c(1) Best Practices **How do you share best practices in your organization?** 4.1c(2) Future Performance **How do you project your organization's future performance?**

(Continued)

Table 4.4 Summary of key approaches recommended to meet overall requirements of Category 4 *(continued)*.

Area to address	Recommended key approach	Overall requirements
4.1c Performance Improvement *(continued)*	• Product or service offerings (3.2a) • Customer satisfaction (3.1b) • Customer relationships (3.2b) • The workforce environment (5.1a/b) • Workforce engagement [5.2a(1-3)] • Workforce performance [5.2a(4)] • GLERCAP processes (1.2, see Chapter 5) • Safety and Emergency Preparedness (6.2c)	4.1c(3) Continuous Improvement and Innovation **How do you use findings from performance reviews (4.1b) to develop priorities for continuous improvement and opportunities for innovation?**
4.2a Organizational Knowledge	**Knowledge Management Process** Includes the methods used to: • Identify, collect, and assemble knowledge • Transfer and use it to improve performance and plans • Embed learning within operations. These methods are often integrated with processes for: • Leadership System [1.1a] • Strategic Planning [2.1a] • Action Planning [2.2a] • Voice of the Customer [3.1a] • Product/Service Innovation [3.2a] • Customer Relationship Management [3.2b] • Scorecard Analysis, Review, Improvement [4.1b/c] • Best practice sharing [4.1c(1)] • Workforce Performance Management [5.2a] • Workforce Learning and Development [5.2b] • Process Design and Improvement Process [6.1a/b] • Innovation Management [6.1c] • Supply chain management [6.2b]	4.2a(1) Knowledge Management **How do you manage organizational knowledge?** 4.2a(2) Organizational Learning **How do you use your knowledge and resources to embed learning in the way your organization operates?**

(Continued)

Table 4.4 Summary of key approaches recommended to meet overall requirements of Category 4 *(continued).*

Area to address	Recommended key approach	Overall requirements
4.2b Data, Information, and Information Technology	**Data/Info, Hardware/Software Management** Includes the organization's Information Technology processes (e.g., Service Design, Transition, Operation, Improvement) and the specific methods used to ensure and improve the: • Quality of data and information • Security of data and information • Availability of data and information • Quality of hardware and software • Emergency availability of data and information, hardware and software	4.2b(1) Data and Information Quality **How do you verify and ensure the quality of organizational data and information?** 4.2b(2) Data and Information Security **How do ensure the security of sensitive or privileged data and information?** 4.2b(3) Data and Information Availability **How do ensure the availability of organizational data and information?** 4.2b(4) Hardware and Software Properties **How do ensure that hardware and software are reliable, secure, and user-friendly?**
	Aligns with the Emergency Preparedness Process [6.2c(2)]	4.2b(5) Emergency Availability **In the event of an emergency, how do you ensure that hardware and software systems and data and information continue to be secure and available to effectively serve customers and business needs?**

WORKFORCE

Table 4.5 Summary of key approaches recommended to meet overall requirements of Category 5.

Area to address	Recommended key approach	Overall requirements
5.1a Workforce capability and capacity	**Workforce Planning Process** The process used to assess the organization's needs and develop plans to prepare the workforce for changes in: • Capabilities – what skills we need? • Capacity – how many staff we need? Workforce capability and capacity assessment provides the key information inputs used to develop Workforce Plans [2.2a(4)] that support achievement of strategic objectives and goals (2.1b) and action plans (2.2a). Workforce Plans also inform priorities for change or improvement within other key approaches in 5.1 and 5.2 such as hiring, training, benefits administration, etc.	5.1a(1) Capability and Capacity **How do you assess your workforce capability and capacity needs?** 2.2a(4) Workforce Plans **What are key workforce plans to support short- and longer-term strategic objectives and action plans?**
	5.1a Workforce Planning can include the approach for **workforce change management** or change can be managed as a separate process. In either case, workforce change management should be aligned with: • 1.1b Senior Leader Communication Process • 2.1a Strategic Planning Process • 5.1a and 2.2a(4) Workforce Plans • 4.1b/c Scorecard Analysis, Review, and Improvement • 5.2b Learning and Development System • 6.1a/b Process Design and Improvement • 6.1c Innovation Management	5.1a(4) Workforce Change Management **How do you prepare your workforce for changing capability and capacity needs?**

(Continued)

Table 4.5 Summary of key approaches recommended to meet overall requirements of Category 5 *(continued)*.

Area to address	Recommended key approach	Overall requirements
5.1a Workforce capability and capacity *(continued)*	The need for **Organizational redesign or restructuring** [5.1a(3)] is one specific type of change that could be identified through: • Strategic Planning (2.1a) • Work System Evaluation [2.1a(4)] • Workforce Change Management [5.1a(4)] • Workforce Planning [5.1a(1), 2.2a(4)] • Process Design and Improvement Process [6.1a/b] • Innovation Management [6.1c] • Supply chain management [6.2b]	5.1a(3) Work Accomplishment **How do you organize and manage your workforce?**
	Workforce Recruitment & Retention Process The processes used to recruit, hire, place, and retain new members of the workforce. This approach is used to address capability and capacity needs identified via 5.1a Workforce Planning Process.	5.1a(2) New Workforce Members **How do you recruit, hire, place, and retain new workforce members?**
5.1b Workforce Climate	**Workplace HSSA (Health, Safety, Security, and Accessibility) Program [5.1b(1)]** Includes the processes, measures, and goals used to ensure and improve workforce: • Health, • Safety [per 6.2c(1)], • Security, and • Workplace accessibility. Organizations must decide whether workforce safety will be addressed through 5.1b Workplace HSSA or 6.2c Safety and Emergency Preparedness.	5.1b(1) Workplace Environment **How do you ensure workplace health, security, and accessibility for the workforce?** *Other related requirements* 6.2c(1) Safety **How do you provide a safe operating environment?**

(Continued)

Table 4.5 Summary of key approaches recommended to meet overall requirements of Category 5 *(continued)*.

Area to address	Recommended key approach	Overall requirements	
5.1b Workforce Climate *(continued)*	**Workforce Benefits Management [5.1b(2)]** This includes the methods used to: • Determine the needs of the workforce and • Provide key benefits and support services to meet workforce needs.	5.1b(2	Workforce Benefits and Policies **How do you support your workforce via services, benefits, and policies?**
5.2a Workforce Engagement and Performance	**Workforce Engagement Management process [5.2a(2-3)]** The process used to measure workforce engagement and satisfaction and use findings from these assessments to: • Determine key drivers of engagement [per 5.2a(2)], • Develop and implement plans to improve workforce engagement and business results. Process should align with 5.1a Workforce Planning.	5.2a(2) 5.2a(3)	Drivers of Engagement **How do you determine the key drivers of workforce engagement?** Assessment of Engagement **How do you assess workforce engagement?**
	Workforce Performance Management Process [5.2a(1,4)] The process to engage the workforce in improvement and innovation. It typically includes a performance evaluation or appraisal method that is used with individuals to: • Set goals, standards, expectations • Evaluate performance • Coach and provide feedback • Compensate, reward, recognize, and • Develop skills and capabilities (5.2b). The approach used here should align with processes for: • Scorecard Development/Update [4.1a] • Goal Setting [2.2a(6)] • Action Planning [2.2a] • Scorecard Analysis, Review, Improvement [4.1b/c]	5.2a(1) 5.2a(4)	Organizational Culture **How do you foster an organizational culture that is characterized by open communication, high performance, and an engaged workforce?** Performance Management **How does your workforce performance management system support high performance and workforce engagement?**

(Continued)

Table 4.5 Summary of key approaches recommended to meet overall requirements of Category 5 *(continued)*.

Area to address	Recommended key approach	Overall requirements
5.2b Workforce and Leader Development	**Learning & Development System** The process or methods used to determine individual and organizational learning needs and provide staff with training or development to meet the identified needs. This approach is used to address: • Capability needs identified via Workforce Planning Process [5.1a] • Workforce and leadership development needs identified via Workforce Performance Management process [5.2a] • Leadership development needs identified via the Governance and Leadership Improvement Process [1.2a]	5.2b(1) Learning and Development System **How does your learning and development system support the organization's needs and the personal development of workforce members, managers, leaders?**
	The evaluation of L&D effectiveness should align with the Workforce Engagement Process [5.2a] in order to correlate learning and development outcomes with findings from workforce engagement assessments and key business results to identify opportunities for improvement.	5.2b(2) Learning and Development Effectiveness **How do you evaluate the effectiveness and efficiency of your learning and development system?**
	Succession Planning Program [5.2b(3)] The process or methods used to evaluate talent, identify succession candidates for leadership positions, and develop and implement plans to meet future organizational leadership needs identified through leadership performance evaluation [1.2a(2)] and learning and development system needs assessment [5.2b(1)]. This approach aligns with: • Workforce Planning [5.1a] • Workforce Performance Management Process [5.2a(1,4)] • Governance and Leadership Improvement [1.2a] • Learning and Development system [5.2b]	5.2b(3) Career Progression **How do you manage career progression for your organization?**

(Continued)

OPERATIONS

Table 4.6 Summary of key approaches recommended to meet overall requirements of Category 6.

Area to address	Recommended key approach	Overall requirements
6.1a Product/service and process design	**Process Design and Improvement Process (PDIP)** The approach used to design, manage, and improve key work processes and support processes. It typically includes steps to: • Determine key processes • Determine key requirements of the process • Design the process to meet requirements • Implement, monitor and control the process through the use of in-process and outcome measures • Identify opportunities and take action to improve key work processes This approach should align with the continuous improvement component of the Scorecard Review and Improvement Process [4.1b/c]. It may utilize elements of or closely align with other similar processes such as: • Scorecard Development/Update [4.1a] • Goal Setting [2.2a(6)] • Action Planning [2.2a] • Innovation Management [6.1c] • Supply chain management [6.2b] Note that design of new products/services/programs is accomplished through the 3.2a Product Service Innovation Process (PSIP). Any new or modified products/services that result from PSIP flow directly into PDIP so that the associated work processes can be designed to produce/deliver the new or modified products and services. For this reason there must be a clear and well-defined linkage between the processes for design of: • Products/services [3.2a PSIP] • Work processes [6.1a/b PDIP]	6.1a(1) Process Requirements **How do you determine key work process requirements?** 6.1a(2) Design Concepts **How do you design your work processes to meet requirements?**

(Continued)

Table 4.6 Summary of key approaches recommended to meet overall requirements of Category 6 *(continued)*.

Area to address	Recommended key approach	Overall requirements
6.1b Process Management	Some organizations use separate approaches to: • Design and implement work processes • Manage and control work processes • Improve work processes Since many organizations lack well-defined processes to meet these requirements at the beginning of their journey, the recommended **Process Design and Improvement Process (PDIP)** encompasses all three (design, manage, improve) and can be refined over time to meet the organization's needs. Often rigorous application of the PDIP approach is applied over time: • First to key work processes; • Subsequently to key support processes. In some organizations the PDIP approach may also be used to address the requirements of 6.1c Innovation Management.	6.1b(1) Process Implementation **How does your day-to-day operation of work processes ensure that they meet key process requirements?** 6.1b(2) Support Processes **How do you determine your key support processes?** 6.1b(3) Product and Process Improvement **How do improve your work processes to improve products and performance, enhance your core competencies, reduce variability?**
6.1c Innovation Management	**Innovation Management Process** The structure, process, and/or methods used to ensure that strategic opportunities are effectively managed to realize their potential, or are discontinued to make resources available to pursue other opportunities. Innovation management often integrates steps within several other key processes. For example, you might: • Use 3.2a Product/Service Innovation process to identify potential opportunities in products/services. • Use 2.1a(4) Work System Evaluation to identify potential opportunities for redesign of key work systems or the organization's business model.	6.1c Innovation Management **How do you manage for innovation?**

(Continued)

Table 4.6 Summary of key approaches recommended to meet overall requirements of Category 6 *(continued)*.

Area to address	Recommended key approach	Overall requirements
6.1c Innovation Management *(continued)*	• Use 2.1a Strategic Planning to: – Identify / review potential opportunities – Evaluate each one in terms of risk and reward – Select a few opportunities to pursue [2.1a(2)]. • Develop plans to pursue selected strategic opportunities. This might involve: – 2.2a Action Planning, – 3.2a Product/Service Design, – 5.1a Workforce Planning, and/or – 6.1a/b Process Design and Improvement. • Use 2.2a Budgeting process to allocate resources toward key strategic opportunities [2.2a(3)]. Note that effective pursuit of innovation sometimes requires separate, dedicated resources (e.g., a Project Management Office, Research Center, skunk works, etc.) that operate outside the organization's current key work processes. • Use 4.1a Scorecard Development/ Update process to determine key measures of success for each strategic opportunity [2.2a(5), 4.1a]. • Use 4.1b/c Scorecard Review process to monitor progress for each strategic opportunity. • Use the 2.1a Strategic Planning process to evaluate results for each opportunity and determine whether to continue or discontinue.	6.1c Innovation Management **How do you manage for innovation?**

(Continued)

Table 4.6 Summary of key approaches recommended to meet overall requirements of Category 6 *(continued)*.

Area to address	Recommended key approach	Overall requirements
6.2a Process Efficiency and Effectiveness	**Cost Control** The processes or methods used to: • Control expenses • Prevent errors, defects, rework, etc. • Minimize warranty costs • Minimize the costs of inspections, tests or audits • Minimize the impact of poor quality on customers Cost control can be managed as a separate process or it may be integrated within other approaches such as: • 2.2a Budgeting (e.g., budgets and variance analysis) • 3.2a Product/Service Innovation Process • 4.1b/c Scorecard Review Process • 5.1a Workforce Plans (e.g., staffing plans) • 5.1a Hiring Process (e.g., position control) • 6.1a/b Process Design and Improvement Process • 6.2b Supply Chain Management	6.2a Process Efficiency and Effectiveness **How do you control the overall costs of your operations?**
6.2b Supply-Chain Management	**Supply Chain Management** Process used to: • Select qualified suppliers • Evaluate their performance • Provide feedback • Deal with poorly performing suppliers. Supply chain management often involves: • Developing an inventory of all suppliers • Evaluation of suppliers in terms of their current/future impact on quality, cost, achievement of strategic objectives and action plans, etc. • Tier suppliers based on impact • Apply different approaches to manage each tier within the supplier base	6.2b Supply-Chain Management **How do you manage your supply chain?**

(Continued)

Table 4.6 Summary of key approaches recommended to meet overall requirements of Category 6 *(continued)*.

Area to address	Recommended key approach	Overall requirements
6.2c Safety and Emergency Preparedness	**Safety and Emergency Preparedness** This approach often includes two separate processes, but each includes the methods used to: • Assess and prioritize risks • Establish policies, processes and procedures to manage key risks • Measure and monitor performance • Inspect, audit, drill or test to evaluate the effectiveness of processes • Appropriately respond to enable continuity, recovery and root cause analysis of events The Safety program may be a separate process or included within the approaches for HSSA [5.1b(1)]. Emergency Preparedness process can be included within the GLERCAP scorecard (1.2b).	6.2c(1) Safety **How do you provide a safe operating environment?** 6.2c(2) Emergency Preparedness **How do you ensure that your organization is prepared for disasters or emergencies?**

ACCELERATING THE DESIGN OF AN OPERATING MODEL FOR PERFORMANCE EXCELLENCE

The recommended key approaches provide a starting point for the design of an organization's Baldrige-based operating model for performance excellence. Following is a listing of the 35 recommended key approaches that were included in Tables 4.1 to 4.6:

1. Leadership System [1.1a]
2. Senior Leader Communication process [1.1b]
3. Governance and Leadership Improvement process [1.2a]
4. Compliance Program [1.2b]. Also refer to GLERCAP scorecard in Chapter 5.
5. Societal Responsibility and Community Support process [1.2c]
6. Strategic Planning process [2.1a]
7. Work System Evaluation process [2.1a(4)]
8. Strategic Plan Objectives [2.1b]

9. Projection and Goal Setting process [2.2a(6), 4.1c(2)]
10. Action Planning process [2.2a]
11. Budgeting process [2.2a(3)]
12. Voice of the Customer process [3.1a]
13. Customer Satisfaction Measurement process [3.1b]
14. Product or Service Innovation Process (PSIP) [3.2a]
15. Customer Relationship Management and Support process [3.2b(1), 3.2a(2)]
16. Complaint Management process [3.2b(2)]
17. Social Media Strategy
18. Scorecard Development/Update process [4.1a]
19. Scorecard Analysis, Review and Organizational Improvement process [4.1b/c]
20. Knowledge Management process [4.2a]
21. IT (Data/Info, Hardware/Software Management process) [4.2b]
22. Workforce Planning process [5.1a(1)]
23. Workforce Recruitment & Retention process [5.1a(2)]
24. Workforce Change Management [5.1a(3-4)]
25. Workplace HSSA (Health, Safety, Security and Accessibility) Program [5.1b(1)]
26. Workforce Benefits Management process [5.1b(2)]
27. Workforce Engagement Management process [5.2a(2,3)]
28. Workforce Performance Management process [5.2a(1,4)]
29. Learning & Development System [5.2b(1-2)]
30. Succession Planning Program [5.2b(3)]
31. Process Design and Improvement Process (PDIP) [6.1a/b]
32. Innovation Management process [6.1c]
33. Cost Control process [6.2a]
34. Supply Chain Management process [6.2b]
35. Safety and Emergency Preparedness process [6.2c]

Companion pieces are available from Kilbride Consulting, Inc. for use by KA owners as they begin to define/design the operating model for their organization as described in Step 8 of Chapter 3.

KA Templates

For each of the 35 recommended key approaches, a separate key approach template can be used as an aid to assist KA owners in defining and documenting their organization's key approaches. These KA templates provide instruction and best practice examples to inform the design of key approaches.

Templates serve to accelerate the learning required to establish an effective and Criteria-based system of key approaches that will become the organization's operating model. On the next three pages is an example of one KA template, for 1.1b Senior Leader Communication.

- Page one (Table 4.7) provides a template to summarize the methods used by senior leaders to communicate with and engage the workforce and key customers.
- Page two (Table 4.8) provides a 5x5 template that can be used to define a process for management of senior leader communication methods. The five major steps of the process are pre-defined as a guide but may be modified as appropriate.
- Page three (Table 4.9) provides a template to document the history of improvements in Senior Leader Communication Methods. This history becomes evidence of evaluation/ improvement cycles completed.

Recommended key approaches, KA templates, and the process for semi-annual evaluation and improvement provide an efficient process to address the requirements of Categories 1–6.

1.1b Senior Leader Communications

Approach used by senior leaders to communicate with the workforce and key customers. Owner: John Doe

Key Approach: Senior Leader Communication Process

Table 4.7 A template to summarize senior leader communication methods.

Senior Leader Communication Methods	Owner (of the method)	Audience		Frequency	Involves		Purpose is to:				
		Staff	Customers or key stakeholders	A=Annual Q=Quarterly M=Monthly W=Weekly D=Daily N=As needed	Two-way	Social Media	Deploy Vision & Values	Communicate key decisions	Recognize the workforce	Create focus on action	Enable innovation

Table 4.8 is a template that can be used to define/design a process for management of senior leadership communication methods. This process may be implemented either collectively, to manage all methods, or individually by those responsible for each communication method. Questions and some examples are provided as prompts to guide you in the design.

Table 4.8 Senior leadership communication process sample questions.

(1) Purpose	(2) Methods	(3) Messages	(4) Communication	(5) Evaluate and Improve
Identify different audiences and the purpose/ objectives for communication with each one	Determine appropriate delivery methods (Which methods from the table above are used for each objective and/or audience?)	Develop communication messages	Deliver communication	Evaluate and improve communication effectiveness
Questions answered by this step in the process: *With which groups should leaders communicate?* *For what purpose?*	Questions answered by this step in the process: *How will we accomplish this for each group?* *With what frequency?*	Question answered by this step in the process: *What is the content of the communication?*	Questions answered by this step in the process: *Who/How/ When will we communicate the message?*	Questions answered by this step in the process: *Is it working?* *How can we improve?*

History of Improvement

Table 4.9 is a template that can be used to document the history of improvement in each key approach. This summarizes changes made as a result of each cycle of evaluation and improvement in the key approach. It provides award examiners with evidence of systematic improvement in the key approach.

Table 4.9 A template to document the history of improvements in senior leader communication methods.

Year	Improvements Implemented
2011	
2012	
2013	
2014	
Jan 2015	
July 2015	
Jan 2016	
July 2016	

5

Requirements for Category 7 Results

CATEGORY 7 RESULTS ARE USUALLY AN AFTERTHOUGHT

The directions in Chapter 4 were to design and implement an operating model for performance excellence based on the 35 key approaches in Tables 4.1 to 4.6. For those committed to the journey, it is important to spend time early in this process to ensure that some of the key approaches for planning and measurement are aligned with the results requirements in Category 7. Many organizations fail to do so and find themselves retracing their steps and revising their key approaches in years three and four.

The reason is that for most organizations, the journey typically begins with a small group of leaders spending time to develop a first application that is primarily focused on describing the processes they use to meet the requirements of Categories 1–6. In the final weeks before the deadline to submit the application, they attempt to pull together some charts and graphs that allow them to have "at least something" for the items in Category 7.

Though less than ideal, this approach can achieve the desired outcome if the Category 7 opportunities for improvement (OFIs) identified in the first feedback report are used to redesign the organization's planning (2.1, 2.2) and performance measurement system approaches (4.1a, 3.1b, 5.2a, 6.1b, 6.2b, 1.2b) in order to address results requirements. However, this is often not the case.

The Criteria requirements for results in Category 7 often represent a significant change in thinking about measurement and reporting of results for an organization and its leaders. Many resist this change, choosing to focus instead on improving the processes in Categories 1–6. They assume that this will ultimately produce better results to report in Category 7. While it is true that improvements in the key approaches of Categories 1–6 will almost certainly improve results, if measurement approaches are not aligned with the requirements of Category 7 it is likely you will continue to miss some required results or lack the improvement trends and comparisons required for scores that place an organization in the 50–65% scoring band for results.

For organizations that are committed long-term to the journey for excellence, it makes sense to understand and adapt their approaches for planning and performance measurement in order to meet the requirements for Category 7 results. Doing so will also ensure you have a measurement system that is:

- Balanced – addressing all areas of importance typically found on a balanced scorecard, including products/services and operations (7.1), customer (7.2), workforce (7.3), financial and market (7.5)
- Strategic – focused on key measures that are aligned with the organization's objectives and plans
- Indicative – identifying trends, comparisons, and segmentation that enable a causal understanding of performance and appropriate actions to improve results

LeTCI RESULTS SCORING GUIDELINES

The scoring guidelines used to evaluate Category 7 results are shown in Table 5.2. Each scoring band includes the four LeTCI dimensions (Levels, Trends, Comparisons, Integration) that are used in the evaluation of results. The LeTCI dimensions are explained in Table 5.1. In essence, the results scoring guidelines require you to understand whether the organization's performance is good, whether it is improving, and whether you are outperforming others for key measures of importance to your mission and your key requirements.

Table 5.1 LeTCI for evaluation of results.

LeTCI	Question it answers	Requires you to report results that demonstrate:
Levels	*Are we any good?*	Your organization's current level of performance.
Trends	*Are we improving?*	Your organization's performance over time (typically 3+ years). The slope of your trend data demonstrates the rate of performance improvement or the sustainability of good performance.

(Continued)

Table 5.1 LeTCI for evaluation of results *(continued)*.

LeTCI	Question it answers	Requires you to report results that demonstrate:
Comparisons	*Are we better than others?*	Your performance relative to the performance of appropriate comparisons such as competitors, organizations that offer similar products/services, benchmarks, or industry leaders. It is important to note that the Criteria do not consider review of performance versus internal goals as a valid comparison. Simply put, goals can be set very low or very high, so performance versus goal is not a reliable way to evaluate results. The TC dimensions of LeTCI suggest that the preferred approach is evaluation of trended performance over time versus meaningful, external comparisons.
Integration	*What is important?* • What should we measure? • How should we analyze results?	Results for all areas of importance to the organization as a whole. Results are segmented by products/services, process type, customers/markets, key requirements, workforce segments, organizational units or locations. Segmentation is a key tool for analysis and improvement of performance.

Aim for the 50–65% Scoring Band for Results

The results scoring guidelines in Table 5.2 demonstrate the differences in the scoring bands based upon the LeTCI dimensions. The 50–65% scoring band is highlighted as this should be the aim when redesigning your planning and measurement systems to align with Category 7 results requirements.

Table 5.2 Results scoring guidelines.

Score	Description (for use with Category 7)
0% or 5%	• There are no organizational performance results, or the results reported are poor. (Le) • Trend data either are not reported or show mainly adverse trends. (T) • Comparative information is not reported. (C) • Results are not reported for any areas of importance to the accomplishment of your organization's mission. (I)

(Continued)

Table 5.2 Process scoring guidelines *(continued).*

Score	Description (for use with Category 7)
10%, 15%, 20%, or 25%	• A few organizational performance results are reported, responsive to the basic requirements of the item, and early good performance levels are evident. (Le) • Some trend data are reported, with some adverse trends evident. (T) • Little or no comparative information is reported. (C) • Results are reported for a few areas of importance to the accomplishment of your organization's mission. (I)
30%, 35%, 40%, or 45%	• Good organizational performance levels are reported, responsive to the basic requirements of the item. (Le) • Some trend data are reported, and most of the trends presented are beneficial. (T) • Early stages of obtaining comparative information are evident. (C) • Results are reported for many areas of importance to the accomplishment of your organization's mission. (I)
50%, 55%, 60%, or 65%	• Good organizational performance levels are reported, responsive to the overall requirements of the item. (Le) • Beneficial trends are evident in areas of importance to the accomplishment of your organization's mission. (T) • Some current performance levels have been evaluated against relevant comparisons and/or benchmarks and show areas of good relative performance. (C) • Organizational performance results are reported for most key customer, market, and process requirements. (I)
70%, 75%, 80%, or 85%	• Good to excellent organizational performance levels are reported, responsive to the multiple requirements of the item. (Le) • Beneficial trends have been sustained over time in most areas of importance to accomplishment of your mission. (T) • Many to most trends and current performance levels have been evaluated against relevant comparisons and/or benchmarks and show areas of leadership and very good relative performance. (C) • Organizational performance results are reported for most key customer, market, process, and action plan requirements. (I)
90%, 95%, or 100%	• Excellent organizational performance levels are reported that are fully responsive to multiple requirements of the item. (Le) • Beneficial trends have been sustained over time in all areas of importance to accomplishment of your mission. (T) • Industry and benchmark leadership is demonstrated in many areas. (C) • Organizational performance results and projections are reported for most key customer, market, process, and action plan requirements. (I)

As with key approaches, organizations should aim to achieve the 50–65% scoring band for results. To do so, you must meet all of the requirements of the 30–45% band and some of the requirements of the 50–65% band. Table 5.3 is a side-by-side comparison of the guidelines for each scoring band.

Table 5.3 Key differences in results scoring at the basic and overall levels.

To achieve a score of **30–45%,** report results that respond to the *basic* requirements of Category 7.	To achieve a score of **50–65%,** report results that respond to the *overall* requirements of Category 7.
The results reported should: • Show good current levels • Show some beneficial trends • Include comparisons for some key results • Address many (not all) areas of importance to the organization	The results reported should: • Show good current levels • Show some beneficial trends for areas of importance • Show good performance relative to comparisons or benchmarks for some key results • Address most key customer, market, or process requirements

ICLeT – How to Achieve the 50–65% Scoring Band for Results

Though LeTCI is the acronym used by Baldrige to summarize the results evaluation dimensions, in practice you respond to the results requirements in a different sequence: ICLeT.

ICLeT suggests that at a high level, the approach used includes the following steps:

- Determine your key measures and segments (I),
- Select appropriate comparisons for these key measures (C),
- Collect and report performance for these measures (Le), and
- Review, analyze and improve performance over time to establish improvement trends (T).

Following is a more detailed description of how an organization's performance measurement system can be used to help achieve the 50–65% scoring band for items in Category 7.

1. Use the Scorecard Development (4.1a) process to select the key performance measures that your organization will use to meet the overall requirements for each item in Category 7. The process for selection of these key measures should ensure alignment with the organization's strategies and plans, customer, market, and process requirements. (I)

2. Determine how to collect the data for most of these key measures of performance in order to enable segmentation of results. The type of segmentation (I) will vary by Item requirement:
   - For 7.1a, segment by product/service offerings and key requirements.
   - For 7.1b(1), segment by work process type, location, and key requirements.
   - For 7.2, segment by customer group/market segment, product/service offerings, key requirements, or stages in the customer life cycle.
   - For 7.3, segment by workforce groups and key engagement factors.
   - For 7.4a(1-4), segment by organizational units.
   - For 7.4a(5), segment by key communities.
   - For 7.5, segment by market segments or customer groups.
3. Determine appropriate comparisons for at least some of these key measures (C). Typically, for each area to address one or two key outcomes will be identified that enable meaningful external comparisons. Because outcomes that are externally comparable are often lagging indicators, it is often helpful to identify a few leading indicators that represent the key drivers for achievement of the outcome, even if these leading indicators are not comparable. You will focus on improvement of the leading indicators in order to drive improvement in performance for the comparable, lagging outcomes.
4. Collect data for these measures to determine the current performance level (Le). Consistently report the results for these key measures over multiple periods to establish trends (T). If you change key measures every year, it will be impossible to develop trends. This is why the selection of key measures in Step 1 is so important.
5. Continue to report, segment, analyze, and improve performance for these key measures until you demonstrate:
   - Good performance (Le) and sustained improvement (T) for most areas of importance, and
   - Good performance relative to comparisons or benchmarks for some areas of importance (C).

Comparisons and Segmentation

These five steps provide an approach that includes both comparison and segmentation of results. It is worth noting that an important change in the 2015–2016 requirements for Category 7 is that requirements for comparison and segmentation of results are now part of the multiple requirements, they are no longer included in the overall requirements for items 7.1 through 7.5. Therefore, it is possible to score in the 50–65% band with somewhat limited comparisons and segmentation of results.

However, as shown in Table 5.2, since the Comparison and Integration dimensions of the 50–65% score band do require some comparisons and segmentation, these should be addressed through your planning, measurement, and review systems. More important than their impact on results scoring is their effect on the improvement process:

- External comparisons or benchmarks ensure that appropriate goals are established and often serve as an effective means to motivate the workforce to achieve performance breakthroughs.
- Segmentation enables the analysis of performance data in order to identify root cause, i.e., areas where intervention will yield the greatest improvement in overall organizational performance results.

Use Graphical Displays to Reveal the Data

It is strongly recommended you use graphical displays to report results for key performance measures. This is not only recommended for applications, but also for reviews of performance data. Doing so can embed LeTCI into daily operations and enable both analysis and review of data. Well-designed graphical displays of data can communicate complex ideas with clarity, honesty, and efficiency. As Edward Tufte says, graphical displays "give to the viewer the greatest number of ideas in the shortest time with the least ink in the smallest space.[11]" Graphical displays should tell the truth and report data in an appropriate context.

The Criteria response guidelines suggest that applicants report Category 7 results using a format that provides a useful starting point for the reporting of all performance data. Figure 5.1 is an example of the format recommended for those submitting applications. While it is not expected that all of an organization's performance measures would be reported in the same format for internal reviews as when being included in a Baldrige or state award application, the example in Figure 5.1 illustrates many of the guidelines for effective presentation of results in any situation. These include:

- Use a compact format, e.g., graphs and tables.
- Clearly label the graphic, including the name of the measure, both axes, and the unit of measure.

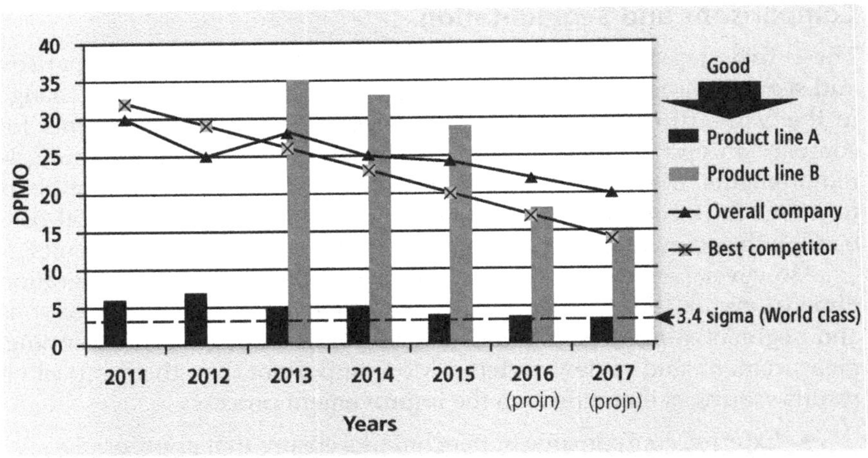

Figure 5.1 Example of results format from Criteria response guidlines.

- Clarify the desired direction of performance by indicating whether up or down is considered "good" for the result being reported. In the example, the down arrow illustrates the desired direction of performance for this result.
- Report the current performance level on a meaningful measurement scale.
- Report the most important results. The example reports defects per million opportunities (DPMO), which is a widely known measure of the quality of manufactured products.
- Select measures of key results that enable external comparisons. There are many ways to measure the quality of manufactured products, but the use of DPMO as a measure enables comparisons with world-class performance, which is considered 3.4 DPMO or six sigma.
- Show how results compare with appropriate comparisons or benchmarks. In the example, comparisons are provided for the organization's best competitor and world-class performance (3.4 sigma).
- Segment results to show the performance of key sub-groups (e.g., customer groups or market segments, workforce segments, product or service lines, business units, locations, etc.) In the example, results are reported for the overall company and for product lines A and B.

- Report results for multiple periods (trends) to indicate the direction of results and the rate of change in performance. In the example, results are reported for five years, 2011–2015.
- To enable trending and comparisons, results should be normalized, i.e., presented using ratios or percentages that make the comparisons more meaningful.[12] This is done by reporting ratios or percentages instead of absolute performance levels. In the example, the reporting of defects per million opportunities rather than the total number of defects normalizes the result and allows meaningful comparisons of the organization's performance over time and with other organizations.
- Consider including projections of performance for future periods. In the example, projections are included for 2016 and 2017 for each product line, the company overall, and its best competitor. (NOTE: Projections are not included in the Category 7 requirements and are not a factor in results scoring until the 90–100% scoring band.)

OVERALL REQUIREMENTS FOR RESULTS

As with approach scoring, the 50–65% band is focused on overall requirements. It is also the first band in the results scoring guidelines where comparisons (C) and segmentation (I) are factors in the evaluation of results. Table 5.4 provides the overall requirements for Category 7 results. It also summarizes the LeTCI factors from the multiple requirements for each area to address and identifies the alignment of each requirement with the related areas to address in the Organizational Profile and Categories 1–6.

It is worth noting that the multiple requirements only explicitly mention comparisons in four areas, namely 7.1a, 7.1b(1), 7.2a(1), and 7.2a(2). In similar fashion, segmentation is not mentioned in four other multiple requirements, namely 7.1c, 7.4a(2), 7.4a(5), and 7.4b. Recognize that even though not included in all the requirements, the early stages of obtaining comparisons (C) and segmentation of results (I) are required in the scoring guidelines at the 50–65% scoring level.

Table 5.4 Overall requirements and LeTCI in multiple requirements for results items in Category 7.

Area to address	Overall requirements	LeTCI factors in multiple requirements	Related approaches
7.1a Customer-Focused Product and Service Results	What are results for: • Product performance and customer service processes? OR • Health care outcomes and patient/customer service processes? OR • Student learning outcomes and student/customer service processes?	LeT – Report current levels and trends in key measures or indicators of the performance of products and services that are important to and directly serve your customers C – Compare with competitors and other organizations with similar offerings I – Segment by offerings, customer groups, and market segments	P.1a(1) Offerings 3.2a Offerings 6.1a Products and key requirements
7.1b(1) Process Effectiveness	What are your process effectiveness and efficiency results?	LeT – Report current levels and trends in key measures or indicators of the: • Operational performance of key work and support processes • Including productivity, cycle time, and other appropriate measures of effectiveness, efficiency, and innovation C – Compare with competitors and other organizations with similar processes I – Segment by process types	6.1b Process management 6.1c Innovation 6.2a Cost control Key support processes might include: 4.2b IT 5.1, 5.2 HR
7.1b(2) Emergency Preparedness	What are your emergency preparedness results?	LeT – Report current levels and trends in key measures or indicators of your preparedness for disasters or emergencies I – Segment by location or process type	6.2c(2) Emergency Preparedness

(Continued)

Table 5.4 Overall requirements and LeTCI in multiple requirements for results items in Category 7 *(continued).*

Area to address	Overall requirements	LeTCI factors in multiple requirements	Related approaches
7.1c Supply Chain Management Results	What are your supply chain management results?	LeT - Report levels and trends in key measures or indicators of: • The performance of your supply chain • Including its contribution to enhancing your performance	P.1b(3) Key suppliers 6.2b Supply chain management
7.2a(1) Customer Satisfaction	What are your customer satisfaction and dissatisfaction results?	LeT – Report current levels and trends in key measures or indicators of customer satisfaction and dissatisfaction C – Compare with competitors and other organizations providing similar products I – Segment by offerings, customer groups, and market segments	P.1b(2) Customer groups or market segments and key requirements 3.1b Customer satisfaction and engagement 3.2a(3) Segmentation
7.2a(2) Customer Engagement	What are your customer engagement results?	LeT – Report current levels and trends in key measures or indicators of: • Customer engagement • Including those for building customer relationships C – Compare results over the course of your customer's relationship with you or the stages in the customer life cycle I – Segment by offerings, customer groups and market segments	P.1b(2) Customer groups or market segments and key requirements 3.1b Customer satisfaction and engagement 3.2b(1) Relationship stages or customer life cycle

(Continued)

Table 5.4 Overall requirements and LeTCI in multiple requirements for results items in Category 7 *(continued).*

Area to address	Overall requirements	LeTCI factors in multiple requirements	Related approaches
7.3a(1) Workforce Capability and Capacity	What are your workforce capability and capacity results?	LeT – Report current levels and trends in key measures or indicators including appropriate skills and staffing current levels I – Segment to address the diversity of your workforce and by your workforce groups and segments	5.1a Workforce capability and capacity P.1a(3) Workforce groups or segments
7.3a(2) Workforce Climate	What are your workforce climate results?	LeT – Report current levels and trends in key measures or indicators including: • Workforce health, safety, security • Workforce services and benefits I – Segment to address the diversity of your workforce and by your workforce groups and segments	5.1b(1) Workplace environment 6.2c(1) Safety 5.1b(2) Workforce benefits and policies P.1a(3) Workforce groups or segments
7.3a(3) Workforce Engagement	What are your workforce engagement results?	LeT - Report current levels and trends in key measures or indicators of workforce satisfaction and engagement I - Segment to address the diversity of your workforce and by your workforce groups and segments	5.2a Workforce engagement and performance P.1a(3) Workforce groups or segments
7.3a(4) Workforce Development	What are your workforce and leader development results?	LeT - Report current levels and trends in key measures or indicators of workforce and leader development I - Segment to address the diversity of your workforce and by your workforce groups and segments	5.2b Workforce and leader development P.1a(3) Workforce groups or segments

(Continued)

Table 5.4 Overall requirements and LeTCI in multiple requirements for results items in Category 7 *(continued).*

Area to address	Overall requirements	LeTCI factors in multiple requirements	Related approaches
7.4a(1) Leadership	What are your results for senior leaders' communication and engagement with the workforce and customers?	LeT – Report results for key measures or indicators of senior leaders' communication and engagement with the workforce and customers in order to: • Deploy your vision and values • Encourage two-way communication • Create a focus on action I – Segment by organizational units and customer groups	P.1a(2) Mission, Vision and Values P.1b(2) Customers and stakeholders 1.1a/b Senior Leadership
7.4a(2) Governance	What are your results for governance accountability?	LeT – Key current findings and trends in key measures or indicators of: • Governance • Internal and external accountability	P.1b(1) Structure 1.2a Governance
7.4a(3) Law and Regulation	What are your legal and regulatory results?	LeT – Report results for key measures or indicators of meeting and surpassing regulatory and legal requirements I – Segment by organizational units	P.1a(5) Regulatory requirements 1.2b(1) Legal and Regulatory Compliance
7.4a(4) Ethics	What are your results for ethical behavior?	LeT – Report results for key measures or indicators of: • Ethical behavior • Breaches of behavior and • Stakeholder trust in your senior leaders and governance I – Segment by organizational units	P.1a(2) Mission, Vision and Values 1.1a(2) Promoting Legal and Ethical Behavior 1.2b(2) Ethical Behavior

(Continued)

Table 5.4 Overall requirements and LeTCI in multiple requirements for results items in Category 7 *(continued)*.

Area to address	Overall requirements	LeTCI factors in multiple requirements	Related approaches
7.4a(5) Society	What are your results for societal responsibilities and support of key communities?	LeT – Report results for key measures or indicators of your: • Fulfillment of your societal responsibilities and • Support of your key communities	1.2c Societal Responsibilities
7.4b Strategy Imple-mentation Results	What are your results for achievement of your organizational strategy and action plans?	LeT – Report results for key measures or indicators of: • Achievement of your organizational strategy and action plans • Building and strengthening core competencies • Taking intelligent risks	P.2b Strategic Context 2.1 Strategy Development 2.2 Strategy Implementation 6.1c Innovation management
7.5a(1) Financial Performance	What are your financial performance results?	LeT – Report current levels and trends in key measures or indicators of financial performance including aggregate measures of: • Financial return, • Financial viability and • Budgetary performance I – Segment by market segments and customer groups	P.2a(1) Competitive position 4.1a Financial measures
7.5a(2) Marketplace Performance	What are your marketplace performance results?	LeT – Report current levels and trends in key measures or indicators of marketplace performance including: • Market share or position • Market and market share growth • New markets entered I – Segment by market segments and customer groups	P.2a(1) Competitive position 3.2a(3) Customer Segmentation

DEVELOP A MEASUREMENT SYSTEM ALIGNED WITH CATEGORY 7 RESULTS

To develop a measurement system that reports levels (Le), trends (T), and comparisons (C) for key measures of performance for overall requirements in Category 7, you must adapt and align multiple key approaches. Following is a listing of the processes or areas to address in Categories 1–6 that must be designed with this in mind in order to produce the results required in Category 7. These are organized into the following logical groups.

Scorecards and Goals

- Selection of key performance measures [4.1a(1) and action plan performance measures [2.2a(5)]
- Selection of key comparative data [4.1a(2)], based on sources of comparative data [P.2a(3)]
- Projections of key performance measures [2.2a(6), 4.1c(2)]
- Strategic objectives and goals [2.1b(1)] that respond to strategic challenges/advantages [P.1b]

Financial

- Key financial measures [4.1a(1)]
- Measures of cost control [6.2a]

Market/Community

- Measures of growth in product/service offerings [3.2a(1), P.1a(1)]
- Measures of growth in customer groups or market segments [3.2a(3) and P.2a(2)]
- Measures of the results of societal responsibility and community support [1.2c]

Customer

- Measures of customer satisfaction, dissatisfaction, and engagement [3.1b]
- Measures for key requirements of customer groups or market segments [P.1b(2)]
- Measures of customer relationship building at each stage of the customer life cycle [3.2b(1)]
- Use of key customer data [4.1a(3)]

Operations

- Measures of product/service performance versus key requirements [6.1a, P.1a(1), P.1b(2)]
- Measures of key work processes [6.1b(1)], including both in-process and outcome measures
- Measures of key support processes [6.1b(2)]

Suppliers

- Measures of the performance of key suppliers [6.2b, P.1b(3)]

Workforce [P.1a(3)]

- Measures of workforce capability and capacity [5.1a]
- Measures of workforce safety [6.2c(1)], and workforce health, security, and accessibility [5.1b(1)]
- Measures of workforce benefits [5.1b(2)]
- Measures of workforce engagement and satisfaction [5.2a(2-3)]
- Measures of workforce and leader development [5.2b]
- Measures of senior leader communication and engagement with workforce and customers [1.1a/b]

GLERCAP (*G*overnance, *L*egal, *E*thical, *R*egulatory *C*ompliance, *A*ccreditation, and Emergency *P*reparedness)

- Measures of governance and fiscal accountability [1.2a(1), P.1b(1)]
- Measures of regulatory and legal requirements and risks of products and operations [1.2b(1), P.1a(5)]
- Measures of ethical behavior [1.2b(2)]
- Measures of emergency preparedness [6.2c(2), 4.2a(5)]

All except the last grouping (GLERCAP) are managed by developing scorecards aligned with the organization's value chain. This approach will be described in the next section. First, a brief explanation of the GLERCAP scorecard concept is provided.

GLERCAP – A Risk Scorecard to Meet Requirements of 7.4a

Item 1.2 includes key approaches for governance, legal and ethical behavior, and regulatory compliance. The multiple requirements for 1.2b include identification of key processes, measures, and goals. Results Item 7.4a is used to report results for most of these measures. The measures used for 1.2a/b generally have one key characteristic in common. They are all related to the management of risk.

It is worth making a distinction between those key results associated with risks that you *monitor* and those key results that you *manage* over time for improvement. Typically the results associated with Governance in 1.2a, Legal in 1.2b(1), Ethical behavior in 1.2b(2), and Regulatory Compliance and Accreditation in 1.2b(1), are for risks that need to be monitored. This may also be true for results of an organization's Preparedness for emergencies or disasters as required in 6.2c(2) and 4.2b(5). These risk areas are summarized by the acronym GLERCAP (**G**overnance, **L**egal, **E**thical, **R**egulatory **C**ompliance, **A**ccreditation, and **P**reparedness for emergencies or disasters).

Unlike most other key measures required in Category 7, the GLERCAP results used to monitor risks tend to be yes/no in nature. For example:

- You either received some significant audit findings, or you did not.
- Employees signed the code of conduct, or they did not.
- You are compliant with regulations, or you are not.
- You achieved accreditation, or you did not.
- You have completed all emergency preparedness drills, or you have not.

In other words, the measures of performance for GLERCAP tend to be all or nothing, yes or no. This is very different from other results for key performance measures reported in Category 7. For example, the key measures of customer satisfaction, employee engagement, operational effectiveness, and financial performance are results that the organization will manage over time for improvement. For this reason, it is recommended that GLERCAP results be included on a separate scorecard, in order to provide leaders with a simple way to effectively monitor key areas of risk.

It is worth noting that Item 7.4 is the one results Item with a clarification note: "Most of the requirements in this item do not ask for levels and trends. The reason is that some significant results may be either qualitative in nature or not amenable to trending over time… When appropriate, however, you should report levels and trends."

An organization's GLERCAP scorecard will usually include results for 7.4a and 7.1b(2) but will be tailored to the priority risks or requirements of the organization. The key approaches for 1.2a/b and 6.2c are used to establish and manage the GLERCAP scorecard. Typically this would be a Red/Green scorecard, monitored quarterly by senior leaders and possibly the Board. For results of this type, leaders are interested in quickly understanding whether they currently have any risks that are not being properly managed (Red) and if so, what actions are being taken to correct the situation.

GLERCAP is proposed as a starting point for what should more generally be thought of as a risk scorecard. Each organization will add, subtract, and tailor the concept to respond to their key risks and requirements and do so in a way that best meets their needs. For example:

- Some organizations will not have Accreditation requirements (the A in GLERCAP).
- Others may choose to include Health, Safety, Security, and Accessibility (HSSA) measures on their risk scorecard, perhaps adding an "S" for safety and making it GLERCAPS. Regardless of what scorecard is used for this area, HSSA results are managed using the key approaches that respond to the requirements in 5.1b(1) and 6.2c(1) and these results are reported in 7.4a(2). For organizations where workforce safety is a key factor, it is likely to be managed as a key process to be improved over time. In this case, safety measures would be key indicators within other performance scorecards, rather than monitored on the GLERCAP scorecard.
- Depending on the organization's approach to societal responsibility and community support [1.2c], the associated results may be appropriate for a risk based scorecard. For other organizations, these approaches are more closely related to customer and market strategies and are more likely to be included with key indicators for these areas [7.2, 7.5a(2)].
- Some organizations may also include supply chain measures [6.2b and 7.1c] on their risk scorecard. As was suggested for safety results, those organizations that are dependent on suppliers will tend to more closely measure and manage key suppliers and may choose to address this separately or with operational performance measures.

Organizations that are interested in the GLERCAP (risk-based) scorecard approach should refer to the 2009 Midway application for an example of this type of approach. The Midway example is a LERC (Legal, Ethical, and Regulatory Compliance) scorecard but illustrates the concept. The idea is to have a risk-based scorecard that allows leaders to monitor its key risk areas. This scorecard is separate and distinct from a performance-based scorecard that is used to manage and review other key result areas.

The concept of a GLERCAP (or risk-based) scorecard provides a simple and effective approach for Item 1.2 and a means to report results for 7.4a. It does so in a manner that is useful to leaders and does not complicate or confuse the reporting of results for all other key performance measures required in Category 7, which are for key results that you manage over time for continuous improvement and performance leadership. These are the subject of the next section.

Results Items Span the Entire Value Chain

For the remaining results items in Category 7, the organization's value chain provides a useful starting point to determine key result areas (KRAs) that align with the organization's strategy and address the overall requirements of Items 7.1, 7.2, 7.3, and 7.5. The recommended approach to meeting Category 7 requirements is implemented through the 2.1a Strategic Planning Process and the 4.1a Scorecard Development/ Update process. Once key result areas are established that align with the organization's needs and key requirements of Category 7, the framework and specific key performance measures are updated annually during planning.

USE KEY RESULT AREAS AS A PLANNING AND MEASUREMENT FRAMEWORK TO ENSURE ALIGNMENT

Many organizations take a "balanced scorecard" approach to strategic planning, goal setting, action planning, and performance reviews. However, the traditional balanced scorecard approach popularized by Kaplan and Norton[13] does not explicitly address all the key result areas (KRAs) required by Category 7.

For this reason it is recommended that organizations establish an organizing framework of key result areas that address the requirements of Category 7 and use these within the Strategic Planning Process in 2.1a and Scorecard Development Process in 4.1a. For many organizations, such a framework is referred to as Pillars[14] or Key Result Areas. To establish an organizing framework that directly aligns with Category 7, organizations should consider each stage of the value chain summarized in Figure 5.2.

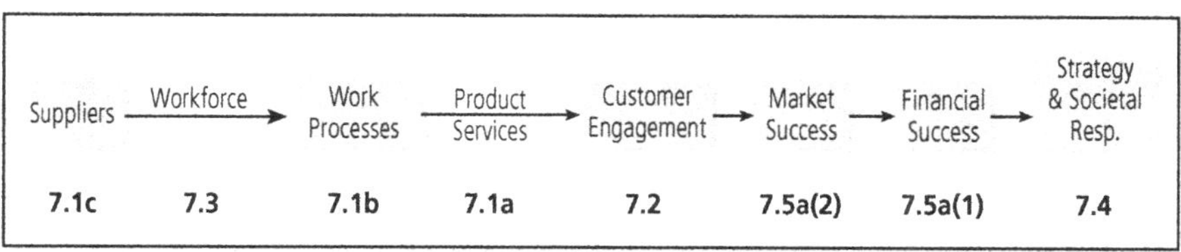

Figure 5.2 Key result areas required by Category 7 identify framework for planning and measurement.

No matter what sector, every organization has a similar value chain that represents a causal chain of relationships. Key *suppliers and partners* (7.1c) provide inputs that are used by a skilled and motivated *workforce* (7.3) to operate key *work processes* (7.1b) in order to deliver quality *products and services* (7.1a) that *engage customers* (7.2) and make the organization successful in the *marketplace* [7.5a(2)].

By managing all of these processes efficiently and effectively you will have *financial success* [7.5a(1)], which will provide the resources that enable you to invest in *achievement of strategic objectives* [7.4b] and also allow you to fulfill your *societal responsibilities* [7.4a(5)].

For education and nonprofit organizations, a different version of this value chain makes more sense. In Figure 5.3, financial resources are the first link in the chain. For example, a school receives *financial resources* [7.5a(1)] from taxpayers. These resources are used to work with *key suppliers* [7.1c] to build schools and buy books. They are also used to hire the *faculty and staff* [7.3] who *operate key processes* [7.1b] to produce *learning outcomes* [7.1a] that *satisfy their students and stakeholders* [7.2a] and make them successful relative to other schools in their *area* [7.5a(2)]. As a result the school is able to achieve its mission and fulfill its *societal responsibility* [7.4].

Regardless of how you sequence them, a framework based on some version of these eight key result areas can serve as the starting point for strategic planning and performance measurement processes. This does not mean you need eight different sets of strategic objectives, goals, and measures. Instead you consider each of the key result areas in Category 7 during strategy development and establish a framework that is appropriate for your organization *and* aligns with the requirements in Category 7.

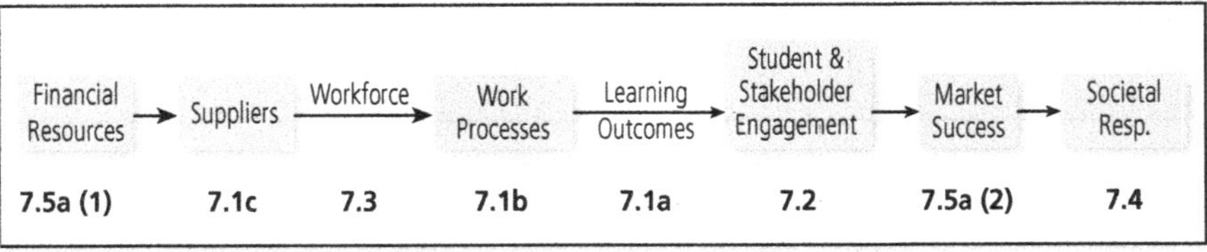

Figure 5.3 Education KRAs required by Category 7 identify framework for planning and measurement.

Most organizations combine two or more of these into a single key result area. For example, Suppliers, Processes, and Product/Services might be combined into an Operational Excellence key result area. Or Product might be combined with Customers and Markets to create a single key result area. Some healthcare organizations combine results for Societal Responsibility and Community Support [7.4a(5)] with Health Care Outcomes, or with results for Market growth, depending on their strategy and approaches.

Not all key result areas from Category 7 are included in this value chain. As previously mentioned, the results for 7.4a and 7.1b(2) are best addressed on a separate GLERCAP (Governance, Legal, Ethical, Regulatory Compliance, Accreditation, and Preparedness) risk-based scorecard.

In most cases, the results for 7.4b Strategy Implementation will also not be included as a separate key result area. Instead, the results of strategy achievement will be represented by a subset of results in other areas to address, namely those key measures within each key result area that are aligned with strategic objectives. In other words, 7.4b will be a summary of strategically important results across each of the organization's key result areas.

The recommendation is to consider each of the key result areas in Figures 5.2 and 5.3 when establishing a planning and measurement framework for your organization. Once a framework is determined for the organization, it is used in the development of plans and scorecards at each level and in each unit. The key result area (KRA) framework is used in step 1 of the Scorecard Development process to inform the selection of key performance measures for all scorecards. Since the recommended approach to achieve Category 7 results is accomplished through design and integration of processes for planning (2.1, 2.2), measurement (4.1a), and review (4.1b), it will be helpful to clarify some of the key concepts to consider when designing key approaches for each of these areas to address.

This is the subject of Chapter 6.

6

Integration of Planning and Measurement Systems with Key Results

Of all the key approaches in Categories 1–6, perhaps the most critical for design of an integrated performance excellence system are the processes used for planning, measurement, and review. As was suggested in the previous chapter, it is important to design these processes to ensure they align with and produce results for Category 7 that span the entire value chain. This chapter explains key concepts for planning and measurement and offers recommendations to enable the effective design and integration of these key approaches.

Plan 2.0 → Measure (4.1a) → Review 4.1b → Improve 4.1c → Results 7.0

STRATEGIC PLAN TIES TOGETHER ELEMENTS FROM ALL CATEGORIES

Design of an integrated system begins with the organization's strategic plan. Item 2.1b asks an organization to summarize its key strategic objectives, the timetable for achieving them, and the most important goals for these strategic objectives. To meet these requirements, almost all Baldrige applicants include a summary of their strategic plan in a table that is similar in format to the one shown in Table 6.1.

TTable 6.1 Example strategic plan summary.

Key Result Areas	Strategic Challenges Advantages	Strategic Objectives	Key Performance Measures (Fig. #)	Comparison	Key Goals Year 1 Year 2 Year 3	Action Plans
Workforce Engagement 5.1, 5.2 → 7.3	SC1, SA2	Achieve top decile performance in employee engagement	Percentile rank (PR) for engagement on employee survey (Fig. 7.3-1)	National database 90th = top decile PR	Workforce Survey (PR) 87th 89th 91st	Workforce Plans
Operational Effectiveness 6.1b → 7.1b	SC2, SC4, SA5	Reduce DPMO (defects per million opportunities) to 6σ level	DPMO (Fig. 7.1-3)	Benchmark 6σ = 3.4 DPMO	σ = DPMO 4σ = 6,210 5σ = 233 6σ = 3.4	Quality Plans
Product Quality 6.1a → 7.1a	SC3, SA4, SA5	Become the industry leader in product reliability	MTBF or Mean Time Between Failure (Fig. 7.1-1)	Industry benchmark 10 million hours	MTBF in hours 8 million hrs 12 million hrs 14 million hrs	Product Plans
Customer Engagement 3.1, 3.2b → 7.2	SC3, SC2, SA4	Achieve top decile performance in customer engagement	Percentile rank for engagement on customer survey (Fig. 7.2-1)	National database 90th = top decile PR	Customer Survey (PR) 86th 88th 90th	Key Account Plans
Market Success 3.2a → 7.5a(2)	SC5, SA1, SA3	Maintain our position as market leader	Market share (Fig. 7.5-5)	Top competitor 22%	Market share 30% 32% 34%	Product Plans Marketing or Sales Plans
Financial Success 4.1a → 7.5a(1)	SC3, SA4	Outperform the S&P 500 average in profitability	Operating Margin (Fig. 7.1-1)	Average for S&P 500 18%	Operating Margin 16% 18% 20%	Financial Plans

The exact format and content of the strategic plan will vary for every organization, but the approach it illustrates is common to nearly all Baldrige applicants. The example shows how the strategic plan summary is used to demonstrate alignment between the Organizational Profile, 2.1b Objectives and Goals, 2.2a Action Plans, Key Measures in 2.1, 2.2, 3.1, 3.2, 4.1, 5.1, 5.2, and 6.1, and Results in Category 7.

For purposes of the example in Table 6.1, six key result areas are shown. As previously indicated in Figures 5.2 and 5.3 in Chapter 5, each organization should develop its own framework of key result areas that align with its unique strategy as well as Category 7 requirements. The example is for a manufacturing company, but other than differences in the content of the Operational Excellence and Product Quality key result areas, it could be representative of an organization in any sector.

For each key result area (KRA) in this example, Table 6.1 summarizes strategic objectives, measures, comparisons, and short- and longer-term goals. This table is an example of the type of information that might be included in an application. It is intended to be descriptive, not prescriptive. Only one key measure is shown for each key result area, though there are often several. Due to space limitations, no specific actions have been identified. Instead the Action Plans column refers to the types of action plans that might be aligned with each key result area and strategic objective.

Also note that the table assumes the organization's key strategic challenges and advantages were previously identified in the Organizational Profile of the application. It is recommended that when first presented in the Organizational Profile, strategic challenges and advantages should be coded as shown: SC1, SC2, etc. for strategic challenges, and SA1, SA2, etc. for strategic advantages. In this way they can be easily referenced in other sections of the application, as in Table 6.1. The purpose here is to demonstrate which objectives respond to each challenge and/or leverage each advantage.

KEY TERMS AND CONCEPTS

Figure 6.1 summarizes the high-level flow for an integrated approach to planning, measurement, and review. This process diagram and the Strategic Plan example in Table 6.1 both use key terms from the Criteria requirements that merit further discussion. As one example, many organizations use the terms *objectives* and *goals* differently than they are used in the Criteria. Other terms used here may be unfamiliar to the reader, or may have a specific meaning in the Criteria.

If you are embarking on a journey to use the Criteria as your organization's framework for performance excellence, then it is essential to understand the Criteria terminology and it is helpful to adopt these terms to the extent possible within your own processes. Think of each step shown in the process in Figure 6.1 as helping the organization to answer one or more key questions. Table 6.2 provides a summary of these terms and the questions each one answers. It also provides specific recommendations for how to address each of these within an integrated planning, measurement, and review system. The terms are organized in a sequence that corresponds to the process flow in Figure 6.1. An understanding of these concepts will help an organization design its own planning and performance measurement system to better align with the Criteria requirements in Categories 2, 4, and 7. As in prior sections, it is expected that the reader will not follow each of the recommendations offered here verbatim, but instead will use these as a starting point for charting their organization's course in the journey to excellence.

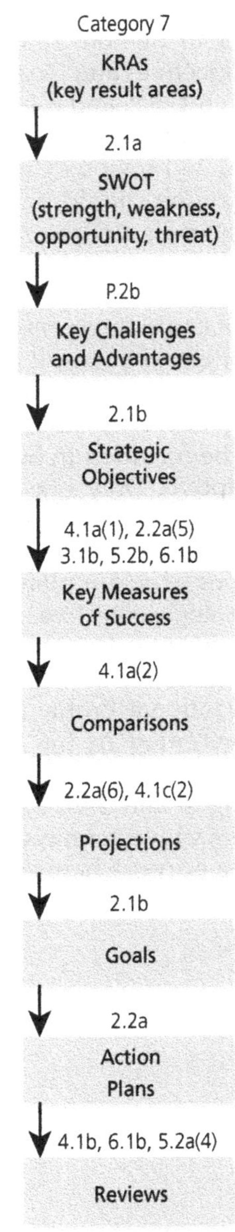

Figure 6.1 Item linkage in Categories 7,2,4.

Table 6.2 Key terms and concepts for design of an integrated planning, measurement, and review system.

Term	Key questions	Recommendations
Key Result Area (KRA)	What is the organizing framework for planning and measurement?	As previously illustrated in Figure 5.2, an organization establishes key result areas (KRAs) that align with its strategy and the requirements of Category 7. Typically 4–6 KRAs are identified and used as the framework for its planning process and balanced scorecard to ensure alignment between Categories 2, 4, and 7 of the Criteria. For example, an organization might identify the following six KRAs as its framework for planning and measurement: • Workforce engagement [7.3] • Operational excellence — includes Suppliers [7.1c] and Work Processes [7.1b] • Product/Service quality [7.1a] • Customer engagement [7.2] • Market success [7.5a(2)] • Financial success [7.5a(1)] The following summarizes how these key result areas might be used at each step of the process shown in Figure 6.1 to align objectives, measures, goals, plans, and results. • For each key result area, perform a separate SWOT analysis to identify strengths, weaknesses, opportunities, and threats. You would complete one SWOT for workforce engagement, another for operational excellence, etc. • For each key result area, review the identified strengths and opportunities to develop a summary of key strategic advantages. Review the identified weaknesses and threats to develop a summary of key strategic challenges. • For each key result area, develop one or more strategic objectives that summarize how you will respond to the strategic challenges and/or leverage advantages. You would develop one strategic objective for workforce engagement, another for operational excellence, etc. These strategic objectives state what the organization must become or achieve to be successful and should be relatively permanent. • For each key result area, select three to four key performance measures that provide a fact-based method to track progress and achievement of strategic objectives. These measures will typically include both lagging outcomes and leading indicators that represent the key drivers of performance for each outcome. • When selecting key performance measures, ensure that at least one measure in each key result area has an appropriate external comparison.

(Continued)

Table 6.2 Key terms and concepts for design of an integrated planning, measurement, and review system *(continued)*.

Term	Key questions	Recommendations
Key Result Area (KRA) *(continued)*	What is the organizing framework for planning and measurement?	• For each key performance measure, develop projections of your own historical performance and selected comparisons to identify current or future gaps. Use these projections to set short- and longer-term goals. • For each key goal, develop strategies to achieve the goal and develop action plans to specify: – *What* actions will be completed – *Who* is responsible for each action – *When* it will be completed. • Develop a schedule of performance reviews to ensure that the appropriate individuals or teams regularly assess progress of the goals and action plans for all key result areas. Each review will assess current performance relative to the key measures and goals, and progress on implementation of action plans. The rest of Table 6.2 describes the approach summarized here in further detail.
SWOT Analysis	What are our key strategic challenges and advantages?	NOTE: From 2005-2013, the Criteria for strategic planning included specific requirements in 2.1a(2) to understand "your organization's strengths, weaknesses, opportunities, and threats." Though no longer an explicit requirement, SWOT analysis (strength, weakness, opportunity, threat) remains a common and effective method used within strategic planning to assess an organization's competitive and operating environment. It is used to evaluate both internal (strengths and weaknesses) and external (opportunities and threats) factors. There are many different approaches to completing SWOT analysis. Regardless of the specific techniques used, the SWOT method provides an effective means to meet the requirement to determine an organization's key strategic challenges, advantages, and opportunities. • **Key strategic challenges** – These can be identified by summarizing the weaknesses and threats determined through SWOT analysis. The Criteria define strategic challenges as "Those pressures that exert a decisive influence on your organization's likelihood of future success. These challenges are frequently driven by your organization's anticipated competitive position in the future relative to other providers of similar products. While not exclusively so, strategic challenges are generally externally driven. However, in responding to externally driven strategic challenges, your organization may face internal strategic challenges. External strategic challenges may relate to customer or market needs or expectations; product or technological changes; or financial, societal, and other risks or needs. Internal strategic challenges may relate to capabilities or human and other resources."

(Continued)

Table 6.2 Key terms and concepts for design of an integrated planning, measurement, and review system *(continued)*.

Term	Key questions	Recommendations
SWOT Analysis *(continued)*	What are our key strategic challenges and advantages?	• **Key strategic advantages** – These can be identified by summarizing the strengths and opportunities determined through SWOT analysis. The Criteria define strategic advantages as "Those marketplace benefits that exert a decisive influence on your organization's likelihood of future success. These advantages are frequently sources of current and future competitive success relative to other providers of similar products. Strategic advantages generally arise from either or both of two sources: (1) core competencies, which focus on building and expanding on your organization's internal capabilities, and (2) strategically important external resources, which your organization shapes and leverages through key external relationships and partnerships." • **Strategic opportunities** – These can be identified by prioritizing and evaluating the risk/reward potential for significant opportunities determined through SWOT analysis, strategy development, or work system evaluation. Most organizations will only pursue a few strategic opportunities at any given time, as these are the strategies that have been prioritized to receive more resources and management attention because of their potential for breakthrough or disruptive change. The Criteria define strategic opportunities as "Prospects that arise from outside-the-box thinking, brainstorming, capitalizing on serendipity, research and innovation processes, nonlinear extrapolation of current conditions, and other approaches to imagining a different future. The generation of ideas that lead to strategic opportunities benefits from an environment that encourages non-directed, free thought. Choosing which strategic opportunities to pursue involves consideration of relative risk, financial and otherwise, and then making intelligent choices (intelligent risks)."
Strategic Objective	What do we need to achieve in order to remain or become competitive and ensure long-term success?	For each key result area, develop at least one strategic objective. The Criteria define strategic objectives as "The aims or responses that your organization articulates to address major change or improvement, competitiveness or social issues, and business advantages. Strategic objectives are generally focused both externally and internally and relate to significant customer, market, product, or technological opportunities and challenges (strategic challenges). Broadly stated, they are what your organization must achieve to remain or become competitive and ensure its long-term success. Strategic objectives set your organization's longer-term directions and guide resource allocation and redistribution."

(Continued)

Table 6.2 Key terms and concepts for design of an integrated planning, measurement, and review system *(continued)*.

Term	Key questions	Recommendations
Strategic Objective *(continued)*	What do we need to achieve in order to remain or become competitive and ensure long-term success?	Objectives should be statements that are easy to communicate and unlikely to change during the long-term planning horizon, e.g., three to five years. They should be stated in the future tense, as what the organization must become or achieve. For example: • Become the low-cost producer of ___. • Achieve best-in-class designation for ___. • Be recognized as a preferred provider by ___.
Key Performance Measure[15]	What numerical information will you use to quantify results for a process, product, project, service, unit, group, segment, or the organization overall?	For each strategic objective or key result area, select two to four key performance measures that provide an objective and quantifiable way to evaluate whether the strategic objective has been achieved. (If it does not result in a number, it is not a measure.) Key performance measures (KPMs) typically include a mix of: • **Outcome measures** – These are often lagging indicators that are difficult to directly action or improve. The advantage of outcome measures is that comparisons are more readily available because they are typically aggregate, industry standard measures of performance. Examples might include voluntary turnover, workforce or customer engagement scores, overall equipment effectiveness (OEE), market share, operating margin, etc. • **Driver measures** – These are typically leading indicators that have a proximate cause–effect relationship to specific strategies or processes used by the organization to improve outcomes. It is often possible to take direct action to improve the performance of driver measures, but it is typically more difficult to obtain external comparisons for them. Examples might include supplier ratings, staff internal promotion rate, productivity, performance relative to customers' key requirements, defect or error rate, changeover time, on-time delivery, time to market, new product share, account share, sales, or revenues. In large organizations, it is not uncommon for key outcomes to comprise the majority of measures on the highest level organizational scorecard. Some particularly strategic key drivers may be included on the top level scorecard, but more often measures and action plans for key drivers are defined and managed at lower levels of the organization through deployment of scorecards, strategies, and goals. In these cases, driver measures become the focus of division, unit, function, department, or process level scorecards and plans.

(Continued)

Table 6.2 Key terms and concepts for design of an integrated planning, measurement, and review system *(continued)*.

Term	Key questions	Recommendations
Comparisons	How will we know if we are good enough? What are the most appropriate external comparisons to evaluate performance for some of the key performance measures in this key result area?	For some of the key measures identified above, select an appropriate external comparison or benchmark. It is usually easier to identify an appropriate external comparison for outcome measures than driver measures. Seek to obtain comparisons for as many of the key performance measures as possible, but ensure that at least one measure in each key result area enables meaningful and appropriate external comparisons. Benchmarks are one form of comparative data. Other forms include industry data collected by a third party (frequently industry averages), data on competitors' performance, and comparisons with similar organizations that are in the same geographic area or markets, or that provide similar products and services in other geographic areas. **The selection of comparisons is one of the most strategic decisions an organization can make.** Excellent organizations proactively seek key performance measures that will enable appropriate comparisons whenever possible. For this reason the availability of comparative data for each measure must be a factor when selecting key measures. Recognize that goals are not comparisons. Evaluating performance versus a goal is important to assess progress, but goals do not take the place of external comparisons. Recall from Chapter 5 that the Criteria do not consider review of performance versus internal goals to be a valid comparison. The preferred approach is evaluation of trended performance results versus meaningful, external comparisons.
Projections	What is the expected level of performance for each key performance measure?	For each key performance measure, project future performance. Analysis of past performance is typically used to determine the historical rate of improvement for each key measure. This enables extrapolation into the future using simple linear regression analysis. This can be accomplished easily using scatter diagrams in Microsoft Excel, plotting the key measure over time. Projections of future performance can be adjusted based on assumptions about planned changes in the organization or its operating environment that might increase or decrease the historical rate of improvement in the future.

(Continued)

Table 6.2 Key terms and concepts for design of an integrated planning, measurement, and review system *(continued)*.

Term	Key questions	Recommendations
Projections *(continued)*	What is the expected level of performance for each key performance measure?	Even though projections are not goals, they are used to set goals in a fact-based manner. Projections ensure that goals are not what you hope will come true in the future, but have some reasonable likelihood based on past performance and planned changes. In addition to projections of your own performance for key measures, develop projections of performance for your competitor's or other comparable organizations and compare their projected future performance with that of your organization. This is an essential step to identify projected gaps, or areas where expected future performance levels indicate the organization will lose ground relative to others. In such cases, particularly when the measure is for a performance dimension that is critical to your organization's future success, it is useful to set stretch goals. Use these to focus plans on taking the actions needed to significantly increase the historical rate of improvement and ensure future competitive success. Just because a projection indicates you could lose ground relative to others in the future does not mean you must accept this fate.
Goals	How good do we need to be? For each measure, what is the desired level of performance that is required to achieve the objective?	For each key measure, determine the future performance level that is required to achieve the strategic objective. As described previously, goal setting should be informed by both projections and comparisons. If an organization has a long-term planning horizon of three years, goals would typically be set for years 1-2-3. This would clarify the desired performance trend and specify the performance level for each year that is required to achieve the strategic objective. Short-term goals are the goals for year one of the plan. Longer-term goals are the goals for years two and three of the plan. Goals for each year clarify the timetable for achievement of the strategic objective. For key measures where extrapolation of past performance projects a performance level that will be sufficient to become or remain successful, the goals established may be equivalent to the projections. Action plans to achieve these goals can often rely on continuing to operate in a business as usual manner.

(Continued)

Table 6.2 Key terms and concepts for design of an integrated planning, measurement, and review system *(continued)*.

Term	Key questions	Recommendations
Goals *(continued)*	How good do we need to be? For each measure, what is the desired level of performance that is required to achieve the objective?	For each key result area where it is appropriate and sensible to do so, it is recommended that you set goals for at least one key outcome measure to achieve top decile performance (top 10% in the nation) relative to an appropriate comparison or benchmark. By setting a top decile goal for at least one measure of overall outcomes in each key result area, you ensure that you are on course to achieve role model performance that is the hallmark of Baldrige recipient organizations.
Timetable	By when do we need to achieve this level of performance?	Timetables are identified through establishment of goals for years 1-2-3 of the planning cycle. Each year during annual planning, goals for each of the next three years can be updated based upon past performance, revised projections and new or modified action plans. The timing of goal achievement for years 1-2-3 should ensure achievement of the strategic objectives.
Action Plans	What actions are needed to achieve our goals and respond to strategic objectives?	Action plans (2.2a) specify *Who* will do *What* by *When* to achieve the goals for each key result area. A separate action plan can be developed that is specific to each key goal, or action plans can be developed that are designed to address all the goals within a key result area (e.g., Workforce, Operations, etc.) Either approach ensures alignment of action plans with key performance measures [2.2a(5)]. Prior to defining action plans, organizations will often develop the strategies that will be used to achieve the objective or goal. Strategies may take the form of tactics, policies, or processes that are intended to achieve the objective and related goals. Action plans are then developed to clarify how each strategy will be implemented. In other words, action plans define how you will operationalize the strategy. Two different types of action plans are common based upon the nature of the goal and past performance. For goals that are based on a continuation of past performance, business as usual plans are often sufficient to achieve the desired outcome. For stretch goals that require discontinuous or breakthrough performance, innovation action plans will be needed. In both cases, action planning should also be used to identify the resources required to implement the plan and achieve key goals. By developing draft action plans early in the budgeting cycle, action plan owners and sponsors can ensure that they obtain the required resources.

(Continued)

Table 6.2 Key terms and concepts for design of an integrated planning, measurement, and review system *(continued)*.

Term	Key questions	Recommendations
Action Plans *(continued)*	What actions are needed to achieve our goals and respond to strategic objectives?	It is also worth noting that there are different methods for deployment of key goals and action plans. In some organization's the performance management process [5.2a(4)] will be used to cascade goals and develop plans at successive levels. In organizations that have implemented a lean management system, methods such as visual management, unit scorecards, KRA, or Pillar boards may be used to deploy goals to various units throughout the organization. Daily huddles and monthly scorecard reviews would be used to develop and implement action plans or improvement plans to achieve key goals. The key point is that many different approaches can be effective for development, deployment, and review of goals and plans throughout the organization.
Reviews	Are we making progress toward achievement of our strategic objectives and goals? What are our priorities for improvement or innovation?	Reviews of appropriate measures, goals, and action plans should occur at each level of the organization (e.g., Senior Leadership, Divisions, Departments, Units, or Functions). This requires establishment of a system of reviews that defines the schedule and focus of performance reviews that will occur at each level of the organization to track progress in key result areas and identify opportunities for improvement. It is not uncommon to have four to six KRA teams, each with overall responsibility for a different key result area. Each of these KRA teams might be responsible for review of the measures, goals, and plans within their key result area. In addition, specific key work processes may be reviewed and managed using a process scorecard. The system of reviews may also include individual performance reviews that are a component of the performance appraisal process. Performance reviews should be scheduled and the following should be clearly defined for each one: • The key measures, goals, and action plans that will be the subject of the review. • The frequency of the reviews. This will vary based on the frequency for updating and reporting of performance for each key measure. Monthly reviews are common, but some key measures may be updated weekly, others quarterly or annually. • The participants in the review. Each review should include those individuals with the authority and accountability to take action on the review findings. • The agenda or process that will be used to review performance, develop findings, communicate priorities for improvement, and take the appropriate action.

Figure 6.1 and Table 6.2 provided an explanation of important concepts and recommendations for alignment of key result areas with planning, measurement, and review processes. The remainder of this chapter provides additional explanation and recommendations for many of the same concepts. This guidance is meant to inform the design of key approaches for strategic planning (2.1a), strategic plan objectives (2.1b), scorecard development/update (4.1a), projections and goal setting [(2.2a(6), 4.1c(2)], action planning (2.2a), and scorecard analysis, review and improvement (4.1b/c).

GUIDANCE FOR STRATEGIC OBJECTIVES PLANNING

Strategic Objectives (2.1b) – Consider Top Decile as Your Default

The definition of the word *excellent* clarifies that the Criteria are about more than improvement. Continuing success is the result of an organization's performance relative to others. For this reason, it is not enough to be good, or to get better; you must become one of the best.

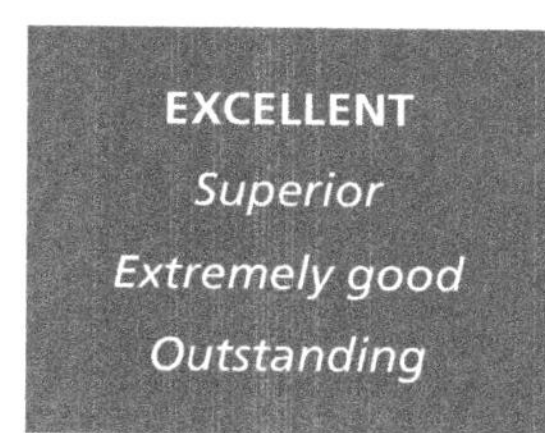

Given this, the recommendation is that every organization's default strategic objectives should be to achieve performance leadership for most key result areas (KRAs). In other words, the development of strategic objectives does not have to be complicated for most organizations. When your purpose is to make quality products, deliver excellent service, improve patient outcomes, or educate students, the development of strategic objectives that aim to be among the best for these fundamental dimensions of performance is very appropriate.

Some organizations find it helpful to develop abbreviated and memorable ways of stating their strategic objectives so this can be easily communicated to the workforce and key stakeholders. Examples include:

- *Top 10%*, e.g., achieve top decile performance in associate engagement, process and product quality, customer engagement, market and financial performance
- *The Bests*, e.g., Best place to work, Best quality or service, Best in market or industry, Best financial results, etc.
- *The Exceptionals*, e.g., Exceptional workforce, Exceptional customer experience, Exceptional product quality, health care or learning outcomes, Exceptional financial results, etc.

The common theme in each of these examples has to do with achieving results that demonstrate the organization is a performance leader relative to appropriate comparisons or benchmarks within each key result area. The reason is simple. In order to be selected as a Baldrige recipient, an organization must achieve benchmark or performance leadership in many key result areas. For this reason it is common for organizations on the journey to excellence to set top decile performance as an objective in each key result area.

Setting an objective to be the best requires that you select an appropriate comparison group to demonstrate leadership. But not any comparison will do. For example, you are unlikely to be considered Baldrige-worthy if your objectives and results demonstrate your organization has achieved:

- The best learning outcomes or stakeholder satisfaction of any school in your district, city or county.
- The best clinical outcomes or patient satisfaction of the two or three hospitals in your local community or market.
- The best clinical outcomes or patient satisfaction among a peer group of hospitals of a similar size within a five-state region.
- Financial results greater than the median for organizations within your industry.

While these examples might show that your organization is better than some others, they do not demonstrate that the organization is a role model and performance leader worthy of the Baldrige award. The recommendation is to set your objective to be an industry or national performance leader, i.e., to achieve performance in the top decile for most key result areas. If you accomplish this, then by default, you are almost certain to be the leader in your local community or markets.

For organizations in the health care and education sectors in particular, a case can be made that you have a moral imperative to strive to be among the best nationally. Do the patients or students in your community deserve less than that? If your family members were the customers of those organizations, wouldn't you want them to be able to receive the best possible care available? The best possible education? If a life depended on it, is the best in this town good enough for a member of your family?

Another reason for setting top decile objectives is to motivate your workforce. People can get excited about working for an organization that is among the best in its industry or in the country. But would anyone be equally excited to work for an organization whose goal is to be above the median relative to a select group of organizations of a similar size and with similar customer demographics?

Setting top decile performance as the default objectives for some key outcomes is also helpful since it can be very difficult to get accurate and meaningful comparisons for many of the upstream or leading indicators of operational performance. The more specific the process is to your organization, the more difficult it is to get good comparisons. Other organizations may not be willing to share this information. Or, if you can get it, the information may not provide an apples-to-apples comparison. For this reason, if you identify one or two lagging indicators or outcome measures for each key result area that can be compared to world class benchmarks or to the best in your industry, then even if you cannot get comparisons for some of the leading process measures, you can have confidence (and demonstrate) that the improvement trends in your processes are ultimately impacting key outcomes that can be benchmarked. If you refer to the example strategic plan summary in Table 6.1, you will see that the key measures identified for each strategic objective were lagging outcomes that can be benchmarked in some fashion to demonstrate performance leadership. If other key measures within that key result area cannot be benchmarked, this is acceptable. But for every key result area, at least one key outcome measure (preferably more than one) should enable appropriate external comparisons.

For some key result areas, top decile may not be an appropriate objective. For the manufacturing example in Table 6.1, six sigma was identified as the objective and goal for product quality. This is not top decile but it is considered to be a world class benchmark level of performance (3.4 defects per million opportunities). The use of top decile objectives often works best for employee and customer engagement survey results, which are usually measured via nationally benchmarked surveys. For other areas, the recommendation is to establish objectives that put you on the path toward industry or benchmark leadership relative to an important key performance measure.

One argument against setting objectives to achieve top decile or benchmark performance is the legitimate concern that such goals can be demotivating when an organization is in the very early stages. For this reason, and consistent with the guidance provided throughout this book, you may need to stage the journey. Begin with objectives and goals that would place your organization above the median, then progress to top quartile, and finally to top decile. But the senior leaders who set such interim goals must maintain an eye on the long-term and recognize these goals as stepping stones in the journey.

Another argument against top decile objectives has to do with necessity. Leaders might ask, is it really necessary for us to become top decile nationally in every key result area in order for our organization to fulfill its mission and serve its customers? That is a question only the senior leaders of an organization can answer and it is one of the most important decisions a leadership team can make. How good do we need to be in each key result area?

It is often true that it is not necessary to be top decile nationally in order to be successful within a community or market. In many cases you can be a market leader with good outcomes and enjoy solid financial performance without being among the best nationally. However, this can also make an organization susceptible. If another competitor moves into your market, or acquires one of your local competitors, the performance level required for sustainability can shift upward rapidly. While good performance may be acceptable for now, there is no guarantee it will be enough to succeed in the longer-term.

Stating Objectives

Strategic objectives should be stated as desired outcomes. They should answer the question, "What must our organization achieve in order to remain or become successful, both now in the future?" Simple examples were provided in Table 6.1.

Strategic objectives should be easy to communicate and likely to motivate. Some effective ways of communicating objectives were suggested previously, including the "Bests" and the "Exceptionals."

Strategic objectives should be stated in such a way that they are relatively immutable over time. This allows you to establish objectives that will not change for the three to five years of your longer-term planning horizon.

However, if you state objectives so they are easy to communicate and stable for several years, they will usually not be sufficiently detailed on their own to meet the requirements in 2.1b to specify your key goals and timetables for achieving them. To address this requirement, for each strategic objective, identify one or more key goals for each year of the planning cycle, as in Table 6.1. These key goals can (and should) change from year to year, but the overarching objective they are aligned with remains consistent. The advantage of this approach is that employees have a sense of permanence and continuity with the objectives, while the bar is continually raised through annual goal setting.

If you survey the applications of Baldrige award recipients you find many different approaches to stating objectives. There is no one right way, but the recommendation is that for each key result area you establish a strategic objective that:

- Responds to your key strategic challenges and leverages your advantages
- Is stated as a desired future state or outcome
- Is relatively immutable or unlikely to change over the longer-term horizon of the plan

- Has direct alignment with key performance measures and appropriate comparisons
- Aims to achieve top decile or benchmark leadership in key result areas

In addition, the multiple requirements of 2.1 suggest that strategic objectives should:

- Balance the needs of all key stakeholders and
- Balance your short- and longer-term challenges and opportunities.

By having key result areas that reflect all key stakeholder groups (e.g., Suppliers, Workforce, Customers, and Shareholders via Financial results) you address the first of these requirements. The second of these requirements can be addressed by establishing key goals for each year of the planning horizon (year one, year two, and year three).

Another multiple requirement is for strategic objectives to address opportunities for innovation in products, operations, and your business model. By establishing stretch goals in key result areas related to Work Processes or Products/Services, you can meet part of this requirement. Innovation of the business model requires a more fundamental re-assessment of key strategic questions such as:

- What will we offer?
- To whom? Or where?
- How will we deliver it?

Strategic Planning and the process for Work System Evaluation [2.1a(4)] are often used to identify opportunities for innovation in the business model.

GUIDANCE FOR STRATEGIC MEASUREMENT

Use the Scorecard Development Process to Select Key Performance Measures

The Scorecard Development Process is an approach that can be applied at the enterprise level by senior leaders of the organization, or at successive levels (e.g., divisions, departments, functions, locations, committees, product/service lines, key processes, or teams) to develop aligned scorecards that reflect the goals and priorities of that specific unit. Regardless of level, the selection of key performance measures for a scorecard should aim to identify a set of measures that is aligned with higher level goals and strategies, and that will serve to focus the efforts of a particular unit on achievement of these desired outcomes.

A framework that uses the same key result areas to develop scorecards at each level is a very effective approach for doing so.

In addition, the selection of measures should consider the alignment of measures across the different key result areas. Particularly at the highest levels of an organization, an effective scorecard is based on cause–effect relationships between individual measures in different key result areas. For this reason it is recommended that you begin with the most "downstream" or lagging of the key result areas and work your way "upstream" to the leading indicators or drivers of performance. This typically means you start with financial or market performance. As suggested by the value chain illustrated in Figure 5.2, financial and market results are caused by successful customer engagement which, in turn, is caused by delivering quality products and service, which is made possible through operation of efficient and effective work processes, and so on. Selection of key measures following this sequence will ensure that your leading or upstream measures are focused on delivering the desired lagging or downstream outcomes.

Within each key result area, you should research, brainstorm, and identify multiple options for possible measures. For lagging outcome measures, it is recommended you seek standard and easily benchmarked measures. For leading indicators you will often need to identify more specific measures that reflect your key work processes and operations. For example, if you were the owner of a fast food operation and wanted to measure "speed of service" during the lunch rush from 11:30 a.m. to 1:30 p.m., there are many different ways to do so. While "speed of service" automatically makes most people think in terms of time measures, Table 6.3 illustrates that this concept could be measured in terms of time or volume.

Table 6.3 Examples of different ways to measure "speed of service."

Possible TIME measures	Possible VOLUME measures
Number of seconds waiting to order, measured by having greeter hand every fifth customer who enters a stop watch that is started when it is given to the customer and stopped by the cashier when the customer's order is placed Number of seconds from order placed to order received, measured using time stamp features of cash register system for every customer order	Number of orders filled per minute from 11:30 a.m. to 1:30 p.m. Number of customers served between 11:30 a.m. and 1:30 p.m. Sales dollars between 11:30 a.m. and 1:30 p.m. Sales dollars per minute between 11:30 a.m. and 1:30 p.m.

The examples in Table 6.3 illustrate that the selection of measures almost always involves trade-offs. Some of the possible measures would require technology at the point of sale; others would likely impact staffing levels. Some use sampling techniques, others include every customer in the population being measured. Some are measuring the number of orders, others the number of customers. Some are normalized (orders per minute, dollars per minute) to enable more meaningful evaluation of performance from one period to the next. You need to consider many different factors when evaluating possible measures including cost, accuracy, validity, etc. And these are just a few of the many possibilities. What is essential is to first understand your objective. What are you trying to accomplish? Then think of different ways you can obtain meaningful data on how successful you are at accomplishing the objective.

Many organizations get waylaid trying to find the ideal measure that uniquely suits their circumstances. There is no perfect measure. Instead you should assume that any single measure will be limited in its ability to provide a meaningful indication of performance. It is the composite of all measures on a series of aligned scorecards that tell an organization's complete story.

For many organizations the selection of measures is less a creative or strategic act and more a research process. In health care and education, for example, key performance measures are often mandated by payers or by governmental, regulatory, or accrediting bodies. Measures may also be identified through review of best practices or evidence-based literature. For this reason, the selection of measures always requires the involvement of subject matter experts with deep knowledge in each of the key result areas.

Evaluation of a Possible MEASURE

When reviewing possible measures for a scorecard at any level, a useful acronym is MEASURE. It can be used to assess the extent to which each proposed measure is:

*M*eaningful	Does it provide a meaningful measure of what you are trying to achieve?
*E*fficient	Can the data can be collected efficiently, using existing systems or at a reasonable cost?
*A*ctionable	Can users of this scorecard take action to impact or influence the results for this measure?
*S*ignal	Will the measure respond and provide a signal when something changes?

*U*nderstandable	Can the measure be understood by those who will review and take action on it?
*R*eliable	Will the data it provides be reliable and valid? [Refer to 4.2a(1) for properties of data.]
*E*asy	Is it easy to update and report at the necessary frequency? Is it easy to compare? (Use COMPARE to evaluate whether a measure provides appropriate comparisons.)

Regardless of the method or criteria used, the evaluation of possible measures should result in selection of those key performance measures that you will include on the scorecard for a particular unit. As part of this process, it is often helpful to determine those measures to include on a *watch list* for future consideration.

A watch list allows organizations to monitor key measures that do not yet meet the criteria for inclusion on the scorecard but are candidates for inclusion on future scorecards. Measures are often placed on a watch list because they are associated with new requirements (either customer, regulatory, or business) and because they are new and lack established baselines or benchmarks. In industries where measurement requirements change frequently, this is an effective approach and helps to meet the requirements of 4.1a(4) for Measurement Agility. The watch list identifies measures that are not included on the current scorecard, but are being monitored and developed for future scorecards.

Follow the 80/20 Rule When Developing Scorecards

Recognize that most of the measures on an organization's scorecard will be focused on the basic activities required for effective day-to-day management of the organization. Typically only a few measures are truly unique or strategic. The 80/20 rule often applies, where 80% or more of the measures on a scorecard can be found on the scorecard of almost any organization in that sector, while less than 20% of the measures reflect the organization's key strategies, competitive differentiators, or core competencies.

Leaders are often disappointed by this, hoping instead for a scorecard that will include only measures that are unique to the organization or its strategy. Achieving excellence is often more mundane than that. It usually involves being efficient and effective in those operations that allow you to consistently meet key customer requirements, while being exceptional or unique in just a few key areas that set your organization apart from your competitors.

As a final check when developing a scorecard, step back and consider, "What are the few key performance measures that truly reflect the unique strategy of the organization?" There are often only a few. But if you find none, then either you do not have a clear strategy or your measures are not yet aligned with it.

Obtain Feedback on Measures

Measures are powerful drivers of individual and group behavior, both good and bad, and can cause unintended consequences. These can range from defensiveness on the part of the workforce to even more undesirable behaviors that can include efforts to manipulate the results. Most readers will have seen instances where new measures or goals are introduced and employees immediately focus on how they can "beat the measure" rather than seeking to identify the changes in their operations that will be required to improve performance relative to the measure. The nature and extent of stakeholders' reactions is often based on how measures have historically been used in the organization:

- If the organization has a history of using measures to "beat employees up" for poor performance, then it is common for employees to be naturally suspicious or defensive. This often manifests in the form of employees spending considerable effort attempting to discredit a proposed measure as unreliable. Their aim is to convince management that it is not a valid indicator of their performance (and therefore cannot be used against them).
- If measures are a significant factor in compensation, including merit or incentive pay, then some employees will undoubtedly try to game the system, i.e., to achieve the goal even if they do not achieve the desired outcome. As an example, measuring "talk time" (the amount of time a service representative spends on the phone interacting with customers) as an indicator of productivity in a call center or customer service environment might lead to some employees spending excessive amounts of time talking with customers about irrelevant things rather than addressing the customer's issue or concern.

It is helpful to consider how performers are likely to react to new measures before they are deployed. By reviewing proposed measures with stakeholders before they are implemented you can often uncover many of these potential issues or concerns. It is also important to understand that by itself, any single measure has the potential to cause undesirable behavior. For this reason it is recommended you review a related set or scorecard of proposed measures with stakeholders to identify some of the possible unintended consequences and determine the best ways to prevent these from occurring. This might include one year on the watch list or a break-in period where no goals or performance consequences are associated with the new measure, until staff better understand it and how they can impact performance results.

Another approach is to include other measures on the scorecard that provide a counter-balance to offset any undesirable behaviors associated with the new measure. In the customer service example, in addition to talk time, you might also measure the number of calls handled and you might survey customers to measure their satisfaction with the representative. These three measures together might encourage employees to achieve a balance, spending enough time on any one call to satisfy the customer, while also seeking to maximize the number of calls handled. If after reading the preceding sentence, your mind is contemplating the possible unintended consequences that could result from these other measures, then you have evidence that there is no perfect measure or measurement system.

Select Key Performance Measures to Enable External Comparisons [4.1a(2)]

The recommended process for selection of key measures is the 4.1a Scorecard Development Process. To also meet the requirements of 4.1a(2) Comparative Data, the process to select comparisons should be included in or integrated with the process for selection of key performance measures. Avoid the situation where you select your key measures, then subsequently try to figure out how to obtain comparisons for them. Consider the availability of appropriate comparisons as part of the measurement selection process.

For organizations setting out on the journey to excellence, the importance of selecting key measures and comparisons cannot be overstated. Baldrige and state examiners evaluate the "goodness" of individual performance results in Category 7 based on trends (T) and comparisons (C). No credit is given for performance relative to an internal goal. The reason is that goals can be set either very high or very low. An organization might set an incredibly difficult stretch goal and come close but not meet it. Or it might set a much lower goal and easily achieve it. Because both situations are common, evaluating performance versus goals is not a reliable way to understand results.

To understand whether performance results are good, you need to:

- Determine whether performance is improving over time (the trend) and
- Whether the current level and trends demonstrate that the organization is better than appropriate external comparison(s).

The emphasis on trends and comparisons is intended to prevent an organization from evaluating its performance based on single data points (the current level) or performance versus internal goals. Either can deceive you into thinking things are going well when they are not. The importance of comparisons is due to the fact that even trends may not reveal the entire story. If you are getting better but your rate of improvement is less than your competitors, it is possible to have positive trends and achieve your goals while simultaneously losing ground in the marketplace and being unaware it is happening. The term *navel-gazing*[16] might be used to describe this tendency, where you focus on your own issues or concerns excessively, at the expense of a wider view. For organizations, the appropriate use of trends and comparisons provides the wider view that places their performance results in a larger context.

For this reason, the process for selection of key performance measures should be designed to enable the evaluation of organizational performance relative to appropriate comparisons and/or benchmarks. In fact, leaders often consider the comparison question first when making these strategic decisions. The following summarizes recommendations around three closely related questions regarding the selection of comparisons and measures and the setting of goals.

1. **Comparisons** *With whom are we competing? How will we evaluate/compare our performance?*

   Given the difficulty in obtaining comparative data for direct competitors, organizations often choose to compare themselves with benchmarks such as top decile performance for their industry or sector. If you are among the top 10% in the industry, you are likely to be equal to or better than most of your direct competitors.

   Ideally you would obtain appropriate external comparisons for every key performance measure, but in practice it is impossible to do so. The more operational or specific the measure is to your organization or strategy, the more difficult it will be to get comparative data.

   As recommended in Table 6.2, at least some of the performance outcomes being measured in each key result area should allow for comparisons. Not only do comparisons provide a meaningful context for evaluation of performance, they also help to identify the need for and motivate an organization to be innovative.

2. **Key Measures** *How do we compete? How will we measure our performance for these dimensions?*

   The second question requires leaders to be clear on how they are attempting to differentiate themselves and compete in the marketplace. There are only so many ways to compete. You can offer your customers something new, better, or less expensive than your competitors. You can make it easier or quicker for customers to access your offerings, or more enjoyable for them to do so. Table 6.4 provides some examples to illustrate how strategy might inform the selection of key measures. You cannot measure/manage everything, so you will need to think strategically when selecting key measures. These examples are meant to be descriptive, not prescriptive. Each group of leaders will need to think for themselves.

Table 6.4 How you compete influences what you measure.

If you compete on...	You might measure...
The variety of your offerings	Percent of revenues from new products Number of products sold per customer Sales revenues per customer
The quality of your products/services	Defect rate Complaints or returns Customer outcomes
The timeliness of product/service delivery	On-time delivery Cycle time (start to finish for a key process) Wait time
The service experience	Customer engagement Retention or referrals Market share
The efficiency of your operations	Cost per unit Yield or throughput Inventory turns Productivity

3. **Goals** *How good do we need to be?*

The third question is answered through analysis and judgment. Once comparisons and measures are established, benchmarking and projections of performance [4.1c(2), 2.2a(6)] are used to establish the goals for each key measure [2.1b]. For those vital few performance measures that are the source of the organization's competitive advantage, goals will typically be set to ensure you achieve and sustain a performance level that is better than your competitors or other comparable organizations. It is both impossible and ill-advised to attempt to be world class at everything. You will need to decide strategically, for each key measure, what level of performance is good enough.

Based on the previous discussion, it should not be surprising to learn that several Baldrige recipients, including Sharp (2007), combine the selection of measures and comparisons and the setting of goals in a single approach. As illustrated in Figure 6.2, the evaluation of each key performance measure leads to the question of whether an optimal comparative database exists. If so, goals are set to achieve top decile performance. If not, a stretch goal is set, e.g., to reduce defects by 50%.

Advocate Good Samaritan (2010) takes a similar approach, but determines the level of improvement that is required for the key measure before selecting the source of comparative data, as shown in Table 6.5.

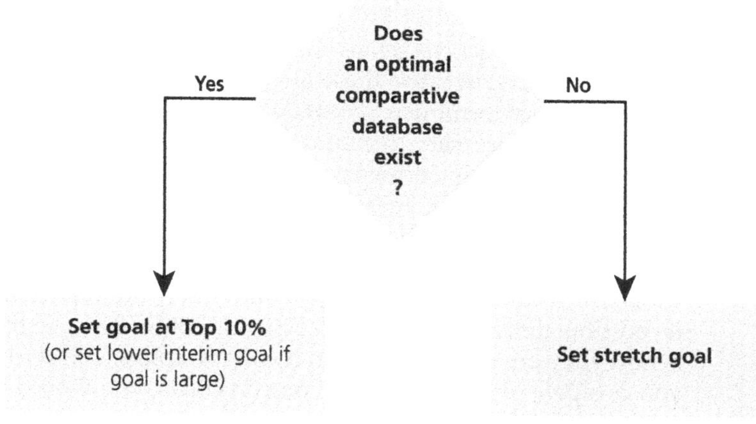

Figure 6.2 Select comparisons, select goals.

Table 6.5 Set goals based on the level of performance required.

What level of performance is required? If...	Select an appropriate comparison
Relatively small, functional improvements are needed	Local, industry, or peer comparisons
Sustained continuous improvement is needed	National top decile
Innovation is required	Benchmark, best practice, or Baldrige recipient

Appropriate Comparisons

The requirements for Category 7 are for organizations to report appropriate comparative data. Results scoring guidelines recognize that an organization will be unable to obtain comparisons with competitors or benchmarks for every key performance measure. Instead, organizations should be thoughtful and strategic about selecting some measures that enable appropriate comparisons for each key result area. Different types of comparisons are described below, organized from most to least challenging and meaningful. This list is consistent with and expands on the approach illustrated in Table 6.5:

- *Benchmark comparisons* refer to best practices and/or world class performance for similar activities, regardless of whether the comparison is from inside or outside your industry.
- *Competitive comparisons* relate your performance to that of your key competitors. Because these are often difficult to obtain, it is important to determine where they are most necessary. They are usually most necessary to evaluate market performance [7.5a(2)] and for those specific dimensions of product/service performance dimensions [7.1a] that are strategic in nature, i.e., the source of competitive differentiation and/or sustainable competitive advantage. The concept of strategic measures was illustrated in Table 6.4. As an example, FedEx would likely attempt to measure its on-time delivery relative to key competitors because this is how they are differentiated in the marketplace. Similarly, if you compete on the quality of your products, you would likely attempt to measure and compare defect rates, returns, or warranty claims with that of your key competitors.
- *Comparable organizations* are those that offer similar products and services. Since they could be located in different geographic areas than your organization they may not be considered competitors. But comparisons with top quartile (the top 25%) or top decile (the top 10%) of comparable organizations within the industry can be a very useful approach. Particularly for education and health care, which are not "competitive" in the same way as business organizations, this is a valuable type of comparison since it can be used to compare your organization's performance with the "best" in your sector. For both health care and education, good leaders often consider it imperative for their organization to aim for health care outcomes or learning outcomes that are on par with the best one can attain anywhere in the country. Do your patients or students deserve less?
- *Industry averages.* These are often readily available and can be somewhat useful. However, it should be obvious that if your

longer-term goals are to be average, you will never become excellent.

- *Intra-company.* Within large multi-unit organizations, it is almost always possible to compare different divisions, units, or locations. While this type of data is often readily available, the difficulty is that one could be the best performer in your company and still be a poor performer relative to your industry or competitors. However, intra-company comparisons can be useful for motivational purposes, as your workforce will usually expect they should be able to equal or surpass the performance of others within their own organization.

As previously stated, since the selection of comparisons is one of the most strategic decisions an organization can make, the approach for doing so should be integrated with the selection of key performance measures. Comparisons should not be an afterthought. Excellent organizations proactively seek to establish key performance measures that will enable appropriate comparisons whenever possible and frequently combine this with their goal setting process as well. At a minimum, before finalizing the selection of a key performance measure, always consider whether an appropriate source of comparative data is available.

Evaluate Whether You Can COMPARE Performance for a Key Measure

COMPARE is a useful acronym when reviewing possible measures to determine whether they enable appropriate comparison. Ideally a comparative database will address most of the following:

*C*ost What is the cost to obtain the comparative data? It is reasonable?

*O*ften How often is the comparison updated? Are updates frequent enough to provide timely data?

*M*any How many organizations are in the database? Is it large enough to ensure valid data?

*P*eers Does it include peers such as key competitors, similar organizations, or industry benchmarks?

*A*pples Will it provide an "apples to apples" comparison? What types of organizations are included?

*R*eport Is the comparison reported in a manner that is consistent with your measurement method?

*E*nable Does the comparison enable segmentation and analysis of the results?

GUIDANCE FOR GOAL SETTING

The value of comparisons and their role in goal setting was introduced in the last section. It is also important to understand the requirements for projections and how this approach also serves to inform goal setting. As was described in Table 6.2, *projections* are expected future levels of performance, while *goals* are your desired future levels of performance. The two are different.

Projections inform goal setting by helping you determine how good you need to be for each key performance measure. Projections are developed by looking at historical performance trends, extrapolating these into the future, and adjusting them based on any known changes that would either increase or decrease the future slope of the performance curve.

The reason the Criteria require projections as part of the planning process is to help organizations determine whether the rate of improvement for key measures is adequate to ensure longer-term success and sustainability. The charts in Figure 6.3 illustrate the value of using projections and comparisons by showing a progression from review of trend data only, trends and comparisons, and trends with comparisons and projections.

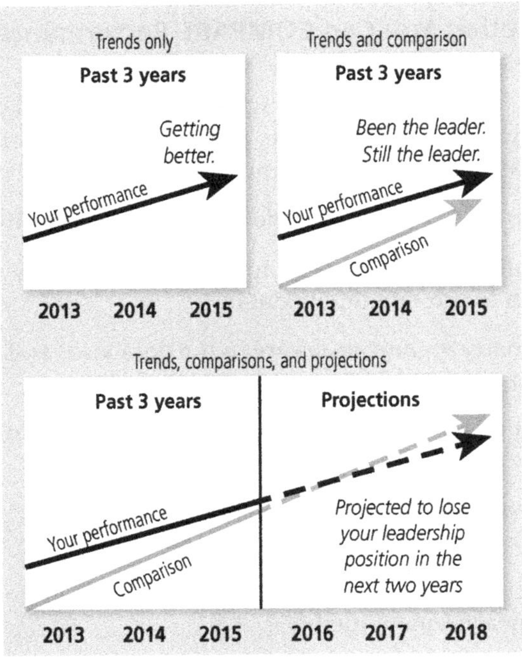

Figure 6.3 The value of projections and comparisons.

The first chart looks at historical performance for the past three years (2013–2015) and shows evidence of improvement. The obvious conclusion is that you are getting better. The second chart adds the trend data for a key comparison. It shows that in addition to getting better, you are better than the comparison. While you are the leader, note that the trend for the comparison also shows improvement and appears to have a slightly steeper upward slope than you do.

The third chart adds projections for the next three years, for both you and the comparison. This makes clear that based on the projections, you will relinquish your leadership position in this performance dimension in the next two to three years, unless you do something about it. Remember projections are expected performance. They help you understand what will happen if you continue on your current path without making change.

You need not accept the bad news and allow your organization to fall behind. Instead, once you identify a projected gap in performance, follow the Criteria and take action to increase your rate of improvement to retain your leadership position. You might:

- Develop strategies (2.1a) and action plans (2.2a) to address the gap.
- Set stretch goals (2.1b) for discontinuous or breakthrough improvement in this area. Recognize that you would be doing so even though you have been improving over the past several years and are currently the leader.

Without comparing projected performance, you may not have been aware that you are threatened with loss of leadership in the next few years. The use of projections and comparisons allows you to identify such gaps.

In essence, they help you determine how good you need to be in order to become or remain successful. As described previously, there are three closely related strategic decisions facing any senior leadership team:

1. Who do we compare ourselves with? (Comparisons)
2. On what performance dimensions do we compete? (Key performance measures)
3. How good do we need to be for each one? (Goals)

This section has explained that the development and evaluation of projections and comparisons leads an organization to identify gaps in projected performance and set appropriate goals to address these gaps. Once goals are set, the next step is to develop action plans to achieve them. This is the subject of the next section.

GUIDANCE FOR ACTION PLAN DEVELOPMENT

Develop Action Plans [2.2a(1)]

Following the value chain model illustrated in Figure 5.2, an organization will often develop action plans to achieve the goals that are set for each key result area. Depending on the key result areas established as your organizing framework for planning and measurement, and the specific key performance measures within each key result area, you might develop one or more action plans for each key goal related to:

- Workforce engagement
- Operational excellence
- Product/service quality
- Customer engagement
- Market success
- Financial success

By developing action plans for the goals in each key result area, you ensure alignment of action plans with key performance measures as required in 2.2a(5). By developing drafts of these action plans prior to budgeting, you enable action plan owners to determine the resources required to implement each plan and ensure that leaders allocate the resources needed to achieve action plans while meeting current obligations, as required in 2.2a(3).

It is worth noting that approaches to develop and deploy action plans can be effective for more than just strategic planning and goal achievement. They can be used to manage many different processes throughout the organization. Action plans can be used to manage your key suppliers [6.2b(2)], your work systems [2.1a(4)] or key work processes [6.1b], your products or services [3.2a], your relationships with key customers [3.2b], or your workforce [5.1a, 5.2a]. Each organization must determine the appropriate deployment of its action planning processes.

Plans Should be Written, Plans Should be Shared

Action plans should be written down. It is not a plan unless it is documented, either electronically or on paper. It is surprising the number of organizations that insist they have plans but cannot show you a document that describes what they intend to do. The value of documenting plans is three-fold:

- It forces the planner to think through the actions that must occur, the timing of those actions, and the resources required.

- It makes the planner's thinking and key assumptions visible to others.
- It creates a record that makes the planner accountable to his/her peers to accomplish the plan.

Simply forcing the planner to logically think through what needs to be done improves the quality of plans. And better planning increases the likelihood that plans will be effective at achieving key goals. It is often the sequence and timing of actions that are enhanced most by the act of writing the plan down. Most of us intuitively know what actions need to occur, but have not fully thought through how long each step will take, which steps must precede others, and when each step needs to be complete for the entire plan to be successful.

In addition, once a plan is written down, the planner can more easily estimate the resources that will be required for its successful completion. By drafting action plans during the same months of the year when you are developing the annual budget, planners (or KRA sponsors) can identify resource requirements and include these within the budget request for their areas.

Another benefit of documenting plans is that doing so allows others to review and inspect them. This provides the planner's manager and peers the opportunity to offer additional input and feedback that can further enhance the quality of the plans. Perhaps even more important is that by sharing action plans with others, the planner becomes more accountable for its successful completion. This is an essential step for a leadership team that is intent on achieving excellence.

How Much Detail? Let Goldilocks be Your Guide

While it is essential that plans be written down, it is not necessary for action plans to include every imaginable detail. Lengthy plans are sometimes used as a way for planners to mask their uncertainty. When you are not sure how to do something, there are two ways to hide this from others. One way is to not write anything down. The other is to provide so much detail that no one can understand what you intend to do. The remedy for both these situations is based on the Goldilocks rule. Not too much, not too little. There should be enough detail in the plan that others can understand what you are trying to do at the beginning of the year, can tell whether or not you are making progress during the year, and can know whether or not you completed the plan at the end of the year. Two pages is often enough detail for an action plan. The review of action plans should evaluate whether or not the plan is:

- *Clear* – Do you understand the specific actions that are planned to achieve the goal?
- *Sufficient* – Do you believe the actions identified in the plan are sufficient to achieve the goal?

- *Trackable* – Are the actions in the plan specific and time bound (or measurable) enough that when the plan is reviewed at different points during the year, you will be able to evaluate progress toward completion of the plan?

What Format?

Many different variations of planning formats, tools, and templates can be used. Some document plans using PDCA (Plan, Do, Check Act) as the framework. Others follow the six sigma model of DMAIC (Define, Measure, Analyze, Improve, Control). Plans can also be developed using Gantt charts, work breakdown structures, or RACI charts (identifying who is Responsible, Accountable, Consulted, Informed). There is a wide range of project planning methods.

The recommendation for action planning is that simpler is better. A simple *What/Who/When* format specifies *What* steps you will take, *Who* is responsible for each one, and *When* it will be completed. This format works well for most organizations, particularly those in the early stages of planning. The template illustrated in Table 6.6 is an example of this format. A few generic actions are included to illustrate the template. Assume the plan is being reviewed on March 1.

Table 6.6 What/Who/When template for action plans.

What Key actions to achieve the goal	Who is responsible	When will it be done	Status (as of last update)
Evaluate options and select a software vendor.	Edward O	January 15th	GREEN Completed Jan. 10
Contract with the vendor.	Connie V	February 15th	GREEN Completed Feb. 20
Pilot test the software in three areas.	Sally S	March 15th	YELLOW In process, may be delayed to March 22
Evaluate the results and make changes as needed.	Edward O	April 1st	RED Schedule at risk due to delay in pilot completion
Train users in each department prior to implementation: • Manufacturing • Sales • Human Resources • Finance	Tammy U	 May 1st May 15th June 1st June 15th	RED Not yet started and may need to delay each by 2 weeks depending on extent of changes after pilot test complete.

(Continued)

Table 6.6 What/Who/When template for action plans *(continued)*.

What Key actions to achieve the goal	Who is responsible	When will it be done	Status (as of last update)
Implement the software in each department: • Manufacturing • Sales • Human Resources • Finance	Sally S	 May 15th May 25th June 10th July 1st	RED Timing may shift but will remain 10 days after training complete
Provide user support.	Tammy U		YELLOW Not started

When a plan is initially drafted, the planner documents what action steps will be completed, who will complete each step, and by when it is expected to be complete. When plans are first being developed the Status column should be blank, unless there are specific issues that are anticipated for pending action steps. The plan should be a living document. Throughout the year the plan should be updated and reviewed, at least quarterly; for most plans monthly updates are preferred. Recall that these are action plans to achieve the key goals for your organization's strategic objectives. It is worth the time to make sure they are on track and achieving the desired results.

Each update to the plan during the year may result in changes to What/Who/When. Changes often include modifying the timing (When) of key steps, and adding additional steps (What) as they are determined to be necessary. Prior to each review of action plans, the planner should also update the Status column so that reviewers can easily determine which key action steps are completed and which are experiencing significant issues.

It is recommended that you use colors (Red, Yellow, Green) and a brief description of the current state in the Status column to quickly communicate to reviewers whether actions are complete or experiencing issues. Note in the example that explanations in the status column are brief. The purpose is not to provide a detailed explanation of every problem or issue that could occur. If that is required, then a risk assessment should be completed, with mitigating and contingency plans developed. Instead, the descriptions should be brief and the color coding of the status column should be sufficient to allow viewers to quickly assess whether or not the plan is on track:

- Red – for actions that are experiencing significant issues or at risk of not being completed on time

- Yellow – for actions not yet started, or experiencing minor issues that are not expected to impact overall completion of the plan
- Green – for actions that have been completed successfully

"Who" Should be an Individual, Not a Role or Function

It is not unusual for planners to initially identify a function or role rather than an individual in the Who column for each action. For example, they might put HR or IT or Case Managers or Curriculum Directors or Department Chairs, etc. It is recommended that you avoid this. For a leader reviewing the status of a plan, what is most important is the name of the individual who is responsible to make sure the action is completed. If something is not happening it is much better to know the name of the one person who is responsible to fix it. Leaders reviewing the plan should not be expected to determine the best way to communicate with a number of people in a given function or role in order to make it happen. This is the job of the individual with responsibility for that action step. This is similar to the SPA (single point accountable) concept that was introduced in Chapter 2.

Time Horizons

The approach prescribed here will result in one-year plans aligned with key goals for each strategic objective. To meet the multiple requirements for short- and longer-term action plans, it is recommended that:

- Action plans define What/Who/When in detail for year one of the planning horizon
- Action plans describe high-level What and approximate When for the next two to three years

The plans for years two and beyond are primarily to identify longer-term resource commitments. The plans for each of these future years should be fleshed out with appropriate detail during annual planning for that year.

In-Process Measures a Valuable Addition

One of the most helpful additions to this template is a column to identify in-process measures. This would be inserted just before the Status column, as shown in Table 6.7. For action plans that are specific to improvement of a key performance measure, such as mortality, reading scores, on-time delivery, or defect rate, the action steps in the plan will often have specific in-process measures associated with them. This significantly improves the ability of both the planner and reviewers to determine whether a plan is on track, particularly when the ultimate outcomes of plan achievement will not be evident for some time. In-process measures might be used to indicate completion of an action, but it is preferable to identify a key performance measure that is a leading indicator and predictive of the desired outcome for the plan as a whole.

For example, in healthcare it is very common for hospitals to have a goal to improve (reduce) their mortality ratio. This measure compares patients' actual mortality rates to what is expected. It is a risk-adjusted measure, where the expected mortality rate is determined based on the particular illness or condition of the hospital's patients. Table 6.7 identifies some common action steps for reducing mortality. It is provided as an example of in-process measures that might be used to monitor the effectiveness of each tactic. These are offered only to illustrate in-process measures, so the Who and When columns are intentionally left blank.

Table 6.7 Action plan template with the addition of in-process measures.

What	Who	When	In-process Measures	Status
Core measure compliance			Percent of patients who receive all evidence-based practices during treatment	
Reduce infection rates			Percent of employees in compliance with hand hygiene protocol based on audit	
Fall prevention			Number of falls per patient day	
Medication error reduction			Number of medication errors compared to amount dispensed	

In-process measures make it easier to track progress toward achievement of a goal during status reviews of the related action plan. They also help an organization to address the multiple requirement of 2.2a(5) for key performance measures or indicators that track the achievement and effectiveness of your action plans. The process described in 4.1a can be used to select key in-process measures.

What else?

The focus thus far has been on the body of the action planning document that clarifies *What, Who, When*. At the top of each action planning document, the following information might also be included:

- KRA – What key result area is aligned with this action plan?
- KPM – What key performance measure is this action plan intended to improve?
- Goal – What is the goal for that key performance measure?

- Sponsor – Which member of the senior leadership team is the sponsor of this key result area, i.e., has overall responsibility for all of the action plans aligned with this key result area?
- SPA – Who is the single point accountable for this action plan, i.e., the individual responsible to develop the plan, update the plan during the year, implement the plan, and ensure achievement of the goal? While many people are likely to be involved in development and implementation of any single action plan, the identification of the SPA is based on the belief that if no one individual is accountable, then no one is accountable. The SPA is often a delegate of the Sponsor, selected to have day-to-day responsibility for implementation of the plan.

This information answers basic questions such as *who* is responsible for this plan (Sponsor and SPA) and *how will we measure* the ultimate success of the plan (KPM and Goal). The header of each planning document might also include answers to *when* questions for the plan as a whole. For example, you might include the date when the plan was developed or last updated, the date(s) when the plan will be reviewed by the Sponsor, and the date(s) when the plan will be reviewed by the senior leadership team. It is recommended that the Sponsor review each action plan with the SPA (owner) for that plan monthly and that the leadership team review each action plan two to three times per year. Reviews of action plans will typically occur at the following times:

- Draft – Review the plan when it is being developed.
- Deep Dive – Review the plan during a scheduled deep dive of the key result area this plan supports.
- Deficient – During monthly reviews of the Leadership Scorecard, any time a key performance measure is deficient, i.e., not achieving the goal, the related action plan should be reviewed to ensure the plan is on track, or to modify the plan as needed to ensure it will achieve the goal.

GUIDANCE FOR ACTION PLAN DEPLOYMENT

Thus far the recommendations have focused on the process used to develop action plans. Recall that the title of Item 2.2 is Strategy Implementation. Action plans have a specific purpose in the Criteria, to successfully implement strategy. Therefore the second key component of the overall requirement for 2.2a is the process to deploy action plans. Three different approaches are generally used to deploy action plans. These include communication, alignment, and ongoing management processes. Each is described briefly.

Communication

Senior leaders are required to communicate with the workforce in 1.1b. The most obvious approach for deployment of action plans is for senior leaders to use these communication methods to tell employees and other key stakeholders about them.

The requirement in 2.2a is to deploy action plans because these are an important means to the achievement of strategic objectives and related key goals. For this reason, the communication of plans almost always includes the broader context of the mission, vision, strategic objectives, measures, and goals that the plans are designed to achieve or support. The content of communications by senior leaders typically focuses on both the future (our vision, strategic objectives, goals, action plans) and the present (our current actual performance versus goals, the status of plans, etc.).

In addition to face-to-face communication of goals and plans by senior leaders, other deployment methods include published documents such as newsletters and memos; electronic methods such as the company web-site, intranet, blog, or e-mail blasts; and the use of bulletin boards and unit scorecards. When communicating with the workforce, senior leaders should assume that nobody has heard the message until they are tired of talking about it.

While consistent communication is essential, it is also important to use common sense. You should assume that anything communicated internally will be learned by others outside the organization including competitors, customers, and suppliers. Examples of strategies that you might not communicate to all audiences include a plan to form a joint venture, to introduce new products that will outperform a competitor, to target new or different customer groups, to close some locations, or to contract with a different supplier. For this reason, it may be necessary to craft different messages for each audience or to draft a public version of objectives and plans that includes information required by the workforce and key stakeholders but excludes sensitive information or competitive intelligence.

Alignment

Alignment is the second method for deployment of action plans and is even more effective than communication. Alignment refers to the processes used to cascade scorecards, goals, and plans and to focus the attention of all units on the key strategies and priorities of the organization.

A simple example of the need for alignment is the situation where an action plan requires involvement from another department or function to complete specific steps within the plan. In this case, alignment might involve assigning these key action steps to individuals within the appropriate department or functions.

But alignment should go beyond assignment of responsibility for action plans. Action plans are a means to an end, which is achievement of strategic objectives and key goals. By cascading key measures and goals throughout the organization and to key stakeholders, you get a multiplier effect as everyone begins to understand the strategic direction and their contribution to the higher-level strategy, even if they are not directly identified as a resource within specific action plans. This is often a key element of the Leadership System (1.1a) in which leaders at every level set goals and make plans for their areas of responsibility that are aligned with the overall objectives and plans for the organization as a whole. As shown in Figure 6.4, this requires leaders at each successive level to ask and answer these questions:

- *What* are the plans, goals, and key measures of the level above me?
- *How* does my area/team contribute to that?

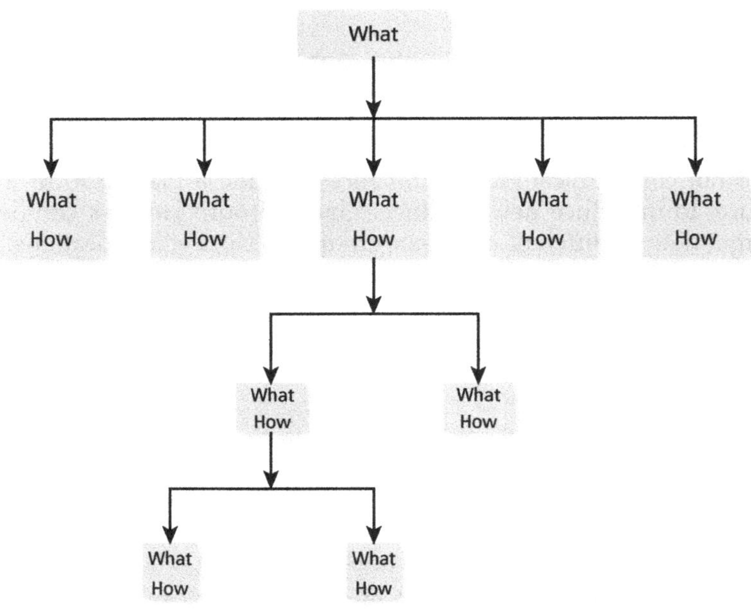

Figure 6.4 Deployment requires translation of plans and goals at each level.

In some cases this can be as simple as adopting the same key performance measures and goals as the leadership or higher-level scorecard. In other cases it requires deconstructing a higher-level goal into its component parts and setting a local goal for your specific portion of it. It might also involve identifying specific drivers or actions your group can take that reflect your unique contribution to the higher level goal or plan. By completing this What/How translation at successive levels, the organization begins to develop focus and energy around achievement of the strategic objectives and key goals.

When objectives, key goals, and action plan performance measures are aligned as described here, the most effective way to deploy action plans [2.2a(2)] is often through the deployment of the related key performance measures [2.2a(5)] and related goals [2.1b(1)]. People often respond more strongly to measures and goals than action plans. Goals create a tension that must be resolved. Actions are the means to resolve that tension. The other advantage to deployment of goals is that key performance measures tend to be stable over time, while the specific tactics or action plans to achieve a goal can change from month to month or year to year.

The recommended approach is to cascade measures and goals to each successive level. By using the key result areas as an organizing framework for goal cascading, you increase the alignment between the scorecards of the governing board and senior leadership team with department and unit scorecards and individual goals. Scorecards for each level should be built using the key approach for 4.1a Scorecard Development.

A Word of Warning

Understand that development of a performance measurement system with aligned scorecards at each level does not happen overnight. It takes time to determine an appropriate set of aligned measures for each level or unit in a large and complex organization. As the performance measures and scorecard at each level mature and leaders gain confidence in the validity and effectiveness of their scorecard, the scorecard development process can then be used to create an aligned scorecard for the next level or sub-unit of the organization.

Patience is a virtue in this endeavor. Too many organizations assume that once the leadership scorecard is established they need to fully automate the measurement process and incentivize everyone to achieve the goals associated with the top-level scorecard. But if the scorecard includes new key performance measures, and the leaders do not have some history with them, it can be wasteful to automate the measurement and reporting process too soon, and it can be dangerous to align incentives with a performance measurement system until you are certain of its effectiveness.

As you deploy the Scorecard Development process to each level or unit, allow some time for the measures and the system used to analyze and review the data to mature. Let each level become comfortable with the validity of the performance measures and the effectiveness of the scorecard in producing the desired key results. Measures often change as the organization begins working with them. If you rush to automate the scorecard, you might find that your investment becomes obsolete very quickly. It is common for performance measures to evolve and their usefulness to change over time. Even worse, if you rush to tie incentives to ineffective measures, you run the risk of driving dysfunctional behavior that does nothing for the organization other than enhancing your ability to reliably produce poor results.

Manage the Plan

The third method for deployment of action plans is to establish and use effective processes for ongoing management review of plans to ensure that goals are achieved. Simply writing the plan is not enough. You must actively manage the plan throughout the year and modify the plan as needed to ensure goals are achieved. Managing action plans and measures in concert also enables you to meet the multiple requirements of 2.2a(6) Action Plan Modification and 4.1a(4) Measurement Agility.

The recommendation is to establish a system of reviews that enables review and management of both action plan progress [2.2] and related scorecard measures [4.1b]. Table 6.8, the planning and performance review calendar, identifies some of the key activities used to manage action plans. These are listed in the row labeled *Manage versus the plan during the current year.* As shown in the table, these activities must be coordinated with the work streams used to close out last year's plan and to develop next year's plan.

A Planning and Performance Review Calendar should be defined and used to manage these three closely related processes throughout the year. Once systematic approaches for planning and review have been established, there will be a repeatable rhythm and pattern throughout the year. The example highlights activities by quarter, but it is best to identify specific months and to adjust dates based on your fiscal year-end. As indicated, the table includes three different work streams that occur during the year. Table 6.8 provides an example of activities associated with:

- Closing out the prior year,
- Managing performance to plan during the current year, and
- Developing the plans, goals and budgets for the next year.

The example calendar in Table 6.8 should be modified to reflect the timing of key events within your organization. It suggests that planning for next year often begins in Q3 of the fiscal year, though some organizations begin this process earlier.

Table 6.8 Planning and performance review calendar.

Work stream	Q1 January–March	Q2 April–June	Q3 July–September	Q4 October–December
Close out last year	• Year-end close for all performance measures • Final review of prior year performance versus scorecard goals	• Complete prior year individual appraisals • Pay out incentives • Evaluate prior planning cycle and identify improvements to implement during the next cycle in Q3		
Manage versus plan during the current year	• All-employee meetings, communication, and cascading to deploy scorecards, goals, and plans for the coming year • Divisions, departments and units develop aligned goals and plans • Employees develop aligned individual goals • Begin review of current year performance versus goals at each level • Begin to implement plans	• Deep-dive review of action plan progress, focusing on one or two key result areas each month	End of Q2, start of Q3 • Mid-year review versus goals and assess progress for all action plans • Adjust/modify goals and plans as needed • All-employee or department review meetings and other methods to communicate mid-year status	• Deep-dive review of action plan progress, focusing on one or two key result areas each month

(Continued)

Table 6.8 Planning and performance review calendar *(continued)*.

Work stream	Q1 January–March	Q2 April–June	Q3 July–September	Q4 October–December
Develop plans for next year(s)			Assess • Update SWOT analysis, key strategic challenges and advantages • Review and confirm mission, vision, values • Update key result areas (KRAs) and strategic objectives as needed Develop • Review current scorecards and update measures/comparisons for each KRA • Develop projections and goals for key measures • Develop draft action plans, budgets, and incentives (if any)	• Stakeholder review of draft measures, goals, plans, and budgets • Finalize measures, goals, and action plans for each KRA • Align incentives with goals • Finalize and approve budget for coming year

Once an organization's overall strategy has been established, it usually does not change significantly from year to year. Instead, the annual planning process is used to:

- Identify any external or internal changes that would require modification of the strategy
- Evaluate the key assumptions behind the strategy
- Further refine and align strategic design[17]
- Update the goals, action plans, and budgets required to progress the strategy from one year to the next

Every three to five years, a more comprehensive environmental scan and strategic assessment can be completed in Q2 to update key challenges and advantages and develop strategies to address them. In other years, the annual planning process is used to validate key assumptions and refine key strategies. But the primary focus of annual planning is to progress the strategy from one year to the next and develop the goals, plans, and budgets required to do so. This approach, which unbundles strategy making from annual planning, fits nicely with a multi-year approach to strategy development and planning.

THE END... AND HOPEFULLY THE BEGINNING OF YOUR JOURNEY

This chapter has provided instruction, guidance, and specific recommendations for the design and management of key approaches for planning (2.1, 2.2) and performance measurement, review and improvement (4.1). These systems are a primary means to align and enable the systematic, fact-based management of strategy implementation and can enhance the management of many other key processes in Categories 1–6. In addition, effective design and management of these key approaches will ensure you produce the results needed to meet the requirements of Category 7 and become a world-class organization.

But make no mistake, world-class does not come easy. The journey to excellence is one of continuous learning, adaptation, and improvement. The Criteria for Performance Excellence are revised every two years to ensure they reflect the current state in validated management practices required for excellence. Consequently, the recommended key approaches in Chapter 4 will be updated with each revision of the Criteria, and the guidance and recommendations around planning, measurement, and review processes in Chapters 5 and 6 will continue to evolve with the Criteria and the learning that results from the best practices of Baldrige recipients.

Regardless of what may change in the requirements themselves, the systematic approach detailed in Chapter 3 will provide a clear path as you begin the journey.

If you are still questioning whether to get started, recall the famous words of Amelia Earhart: "The most difficult thing is the decision to act, the rest is merely tenacity."

IN CLOSING

I am certain that some in the Baldrige community will find the road map provided here too detailed and/or too prescriptive. I admit guilt on both counts.

It is my view that for advice to be helpful it must be specific. If you are cycling from Chicago to San Francisco, you will appreciate more detailed directions than "head west." Admittedly, by considering a specific route for such a journey, you will inevitably discover that others may have a better approach to proceed through the Rocky Mountains. That is how we learn. I have no doubt that as I continue to learn, my recommendations and the road map itself will continue to evolve.

Others may contend that Baldrige is non-prescriptive by design and that each organization should find its own way. This strikes me as similar to the argument that medical school residents should endure grueling work schedules because "I had to do it when I was in training."

As a community, Baldrige and state-award examiners require applicants to have systematic approaches for everything they do, but have failed to provide them with a well-defined process for using award programs. This book attempts to do just that.

My goal is to increase the number of organizations that use the Criteria and state award programs.

My strategy to achieve that goal is to provide a clear and well-defined approach for doing so.

My audience is senior leaders. I know them to be people who want specific, actionable advice and who have no hesitancy to adjust the guidance provided as they see fit for their organization. I trust they will do so.

Notes

1. Walter Kiechel, "The Management Century," *Harvard Business Review,* November 2012. "In 1886, addressing the nascent American Society of Mechanical Engineers, Henry R. Towne proposed that "the management of works" be considered a modern art—thereby heralding the Management Century, when management as we know it came into being and shaped the world in which we work."
2. Walter Kiechel, "The Management Century," *Harvard Business Review,* November 2012.
3. This quote is from the website of the Baldrige Performance Excellence Program. Refer to http://www.nist.gov/baldrige/publications/criteria.cfm.
4. This quote is from the website of the Baldrige Performance Excellence Program. Refer to http://www.nist.gov/baldrige/about/faqs_using_criteria.cfm.
5. In truth, the Criteria do prescribe *What* processes an organization should have in place, but not *How* those processes should be designed for any specific organization. A set of recommended key approaches to be used as a starting point are summarized in Chapter 4 .
6. From *The New Economics for Industry, Government, and Education* by W. Edwards Deming, 2nd edition, originally published in 1994 by Massachusetts Institute of Technology, Center for Advanced Educational Services, Cambridge, Massachusetts © 1994 The W. Edwards Deming Institute.
7. The Glossary of Key Terms in the 2015–2016 Baldrige Excellence Framework defines *systematic* as follows: Well-ordered, repeatable, and exhibiting the use of data and information so that learning is possible. Approaches are systematic if they build in the opportunity

for evaluation, improvement, and sharing, thereby permitting a gain in maturity. To see the term in use, refer to the Process Scoring Guidelines in Table 2.1.

8. My first encounter with CAP-Do was in the book *Fourth Generation Management* by Brian L. Joiner, © 1994 by Joiner Associates, McGraw-Hill, Inc. While CAP-Do is nothing more than a re-sequencing of the PDCA improvement cycle, in my experience it is a good fit for improvement relative to the Criteria. An organization begins the journey with an assessment (Check) of how well the processes they have in place meet Criteria requirements. Each semi-annual review is another Check that initiates a cycle of improvement in the organization's key approaches. CAP-Do is also an effective alternative when fact-based management is a priority. Too many times PDCA is initiated with an idea, which you Plan and Do. After the fact, you try to figure out how to Check (measure) its impact. CAP-Do avoids this problem by putting measurement first. The CAP-Do cycle is initiated by the Check step, which involves some form of measurement or assessment of current performance. An organization can build the CAP-Do cycle of improvement into daily operations by scheduling reviews of key processes or performance indicators. Each review initiates the CAP-Do cycle. This puts improvement on a calendar and measurement at the forefront of each improvement cycle.

9. Following is an example to illustrate the 5x5 process definition method.

1 Take the order	2 Prepare the pizza	3 Cook the pizza	4 Package the pizza	5 Deliver the pizza
1.1 Answer phone and greet customer	2.1 Roll out dough	3.1 Determine oven time	4.1 Fold box	5.1 Determine route
1.2 Write down order information	2.2 Spread sauce	3.2 Determine place in queue	4.2 Put separator on pizza	5.2 Sequence pizzas per route
1.3 Repeat order information	2.3 Cover with cheese	3.3 Place pizza in oven	4.3 Insert pizza into box	5.3 Stack pizzas
1.4 State delivery time	2.4 Gather toppings	3.4 Check and rotate	4.4 Close box	5.4 Drive route
1.5 Pass order to kitchen	2.5 Place toppings	3.5 Remove from oven	4.5 Hand-off to delivery	5.5 Deliver and collect payment

10. In lean management, *Gemba* is the Japanese term for "actual place." It refers to the place where value-creating work actually occurs. This term is used to stress the concept that real improvement requires a shop-floor focus based on direct observation of current conditions where work is done. Refer to http://www.lean.org.
11. From "The Visual Display of Quantitative Information," copyright 1983 by Edward R. Tufte.
12. As described in the Guidelines for Responding to Results Items in the Criteria, it would be meaningless to compare the total number of injuries in a company with 100 employees to the total number of injuries in a company with 100,000 employees. However, reporting the number of injuries per employee would provide a more meaningful result for purposes of comparing performance between these two organizations. The same problem arises if you report the number of injuries over a five-year period. The comparison of one period to the next might be meaningless if the number of employees significantly increased or decreased over that time. But if the result is normalized and reported as injuries per employee during each period, the comparison of performance over time is again meaningful.
13. Refer to *Balanced Scorecard: Translating Strategy into Action*, © 1996 by Robert S. Kaplan and David P. Norton, Harvard Business School Press.
14. The Studer Group popularized the use of "pillars" through their consulting with organizations in the health care sector. Pillars serve as the foundation for setting organizational goals and measuring performance. According to the Studer Group (www.studergroup.com), most organizations use five pillars: Service, People, Quality, Financial, and Growth. The Studer Group was itself a Baldrige-award recipient in 2010.
15. The terms *key performance measure* (KPM) and *key performance indicator* (KPI) are interchangeable in the Criteria. The Baldrige glossary suggests that some use the terms to distinguish between leading and lagging indicators. In this case, KPI would identify a leading indicator and KPM a lagging indicator or performance outcome. However, in my experience, most organizations simply adopt one term or the other (KPI or KPM). When distinguishing between leading and lagging it is common to refer to in-process (I) and outcome (O) measures of performance.

16. The Google Dictionary defines *navel-gazing* as "self-indulgent or excessive contemplation of oneself or a single issue, at the expense of a wider view." Merriam Webster defines it as "the activity of thinking too much or too deeply about yourself, your experiences, your feelings, etc."
17. This is what Jim Collins refers to as the Flywheel or 20 Mile March. Refer to *Great by Choice,* © 2011 by Jim Collins and Morten T. Hansen; HarperCollins Publishers.

Index

Page numbers in *italics* refer to figures or tables.

A

accountability management, 36
accreditation requirements, 110
action plan deployment
  alignment, 151–153
  communication, 151
  ongoing management processes, 154–157
  patience required, 153–154
  planning and performance review calendar, 154, *155–156t*
  three approaches, 150
action plan development
  additional information included, 149–150
  detail level, 145–146
  format, 146–148
  in-process measures, 148–149
  for key results areas, 144
  role responsibility, 148
  time horizons, 148
  who/what/when template, *146t*
  written and shared, 144–145
action planning process, *69t, 71t*
action plans, *125–126t*
ADLI evaluation factors
  feedback and scoring, 14–15
  individual processes and, 14
  Integration dimension, 13–14
  maturity levels, 19–20
  overview, 11–12
  and PDCA, 12
alignment, ADLI and, 13
annual cycle, 42–44, *43t*
application development, 32, 34, 44, 45–47, *45f*, 58–60
application development teams, 32, 34

B

Baldrige Award Program, 4, 27, 28. *See also* Criteria for Performance Excellence; journey to excellence
Black, Gordon, 3
BOM (basic, overall, multiple) hierarchy, 20–24
budgeting process, *69t*

C

CAP-Do process, 29–30, 54, 58, 160
Category 7 results
  as an afterthought, 93–94
  comparisons and segmentation, 99
  GLERCAP scorecard, 108–110
  graphical displays, 99–101
  item linkage, *118f*
  key result areas (KRA), 111–113
  LeTCI scoring guidelines, 94–101
  measurement system aligned with, 107–111
  overall requirements, 101–106
  as planning and measurement framework, 111–113
  value chain span, 111

category integration, 115–117
category sponsorship, 36, 58
category teams, 32, 46
change management, 35–38
Collins, Jim, 4
communication and organizational performance, *65t*
community support, 110
comparisons, *123t*, 128
complaint management, 64, *73t*
compliance programs, *66t*
cost control, *86t*
Criteria for Performance Excellence. *See also* Baldrige Award Program; journey to excellence
  ADLI scoring guidelines, 19
  application and feedback review processes, 25–27
  areas to address, 24–25
  awards and, 15
  BOM hierarchy, 20–24
  building blocks, 24–25
  Categories 1-6, 6–7
  Category 7 results requirements, 93–94
  external feedback, 8
  key approaches, 25–27
  key terms and concepts, 118–127
  leadership triad, 6
  milestones, 15–16
  minimum scoring requirements, 17
  multiplier effect, 13
  non-prescriptive nature of, 4–5
  operating model design, 87–92
  opportunities for improvement (OFI), 26–27
  overview, 6–7, *6f*
  point values and scoring guidelines, 17, *18t*, 19, *19–20t*
  scoring bands, 15–16, 20
  staging the journey, 20–24
customer relationship management process, *73t*
customers, key approach recommendations, 64, *71–74t*
customer satisfaction management, 14, *72t*

D

data/information management, *78t*
data reporting, 101, 133, 161
Deming, W. Edwards, 8
desired outcomes, objectives as, 130
"downstream" indicators, 132

E

80/20 rule, 134–135
emergency preparedness, *87t*
excellence, defined, 127
external feedback, 8, 29–30

F

feedback, 51–53
feedback and scoring, 14–15, 44
first sponsor review and benchmarking, 40
5x5 process definition method, 39, 89, 160
follow-up workshops, 34–35

G

GLERCAP risk scorecard, 108–110, 113
Gemba, go to the, 40, 161
goals, *124–125t*
goal setting guidance, 142–143
governance and leadership improvement, *65t*

H

hardware/software management, *78t*
Health Care Criteria for Performance Excellence, 20–24, *21f*
history of improvements template, *92t*
host site preparation, 48–50
HSSA results, 110

I

ICLeT scoring sequence, 97–98
innovation management process, *84t*
integration, Baldrige definition of, 13

J

journey to excellence. *See also* Criteria for Performance Excellence
- accountability management, 36
- application development, 58–60
- application development teams, 32, 34
- CAP-Do process, 29–30, 58
- category sponsorship, 36, 58
- category teams, 32
- change management, 35–38
- feedback, 51–53
- follow-up workshops, 34–35
- future applications, 58–60
- host site preparation, 48–50
- key approach documentation, 38–42
- key approach identification workshops, 33–34
- key approach owner responsibility, 37–38
- kick-off sessions, 32–33
- overview, 29–30
- road map summary, 60–61
- single point accountable (SPA), 35–36
- stakeholder management, 35
- year one, 31–40
- year two and beyond, 42–59

K

KA check-in, 40
KA templates, 89–92, *90t*, *91t*, 92
key approach documentation, 38–42
key approach identification workshops, 33–34
key approach ownership responsibility, 37–38, 44
key approach recommendations
- customers, *71–74t*
- history of improvements template, *92t*
- leadership, *64–66t*
- measurement, analysis, knowledge management, *74–78t*
- operations, *82–87t*
- overview, 63–64
- senior leader communication templates, *90t*, *91t*, 92
- strategy, *67–71t*
- workforce, *79–82t*

key performance indicator (KPI), 161
key performance measures, *122t*, 161
key result areas (KRA)
- design integration, *119–120f*
- as planning and measurement framework, 111–113
- planning and measurement systems, *119–120f*

key terms and concepts, 118–127
kick-off sessions, 32–33
Kiechel, Walter, 1
knowledge management process, *77t*

L

leadership, key approach recommendations, *64–66t*
leadership triad, 6
learning and development systems, *82t*
legal and ethical behavior, *66t*
LERC (Legal, Ethical, and Regulatory Compliance) scorecard, 110
LeTCI results
- 50–65% scoring band, 95–97
- ICLeT scoring sequence, 97–98
- scoring guidelines, 93–94

M

Malcolm Baldrige National Quality Improvement Act (1987), 4
management profession, relative immaturity of, 1–2
MEASURE (acronym), 133–134
measurement, analysis, knowledge management, *74–78t*

N

normalized data, 101, 133, 161

O

objectives, as desired outcomes, 130
operations, key approach recommendations, *82–87t*
opportunities for improvement (OFI), 26–27, 55
organizational governance, *65t*
organizational leadership, 2, 3
organizational profile, 31, *32t*
organizational redesign or restructuring, *80t*

P

PDCA cycle, 12, 29, 160
pillars, 111, 161
planning and measurement systems
  action plan deployment, 150–157
  action plan development, 144–150
  action plans, *125–126t*
  category integration, 115–117
  comparisons, *123t*, 128
  goals, *124–125t*
  goal setting guidance, 142–143
  key performance measures, *122t*
  key result areas (KRA), *119–120f*
  key results integration, 115
  key terms and concepts, 118–127
  overview, 115
  projections, *123t*
  reviews, *126t*
  strategic measurement, 131–141
  strategic objectives, 115–117, *121–122t*, 127–131
  strategic plan summary example, *116t*
  SWOT analysis, *120–121f*
  timetables, *125t*
points, as milestones, 15–16
process design and improvement process (PDIP), *83t*
process scoring guidelines, *18t*
product or service innovation process (PSIP), *72t*
projections, *123t*
projections and comparisons, 142–143
projections and goal setting processes, *68t*

R

reviews, *126t*
road maps, 2–3, 5–6, 60–61. *See also* Criteria for Performance Excellence

S

safety and emergency preparedness, *87t*
scorecard analysis, review, and orginizational improvement, *75–76t*
scorecard development/update process, *70t*, *74t*, *75t*, 131–133
scoring guidelines
  ADLI evaluation factors, 12
  BOM hierarchy, 20–24
  overview, 11
second sponsor review, 41
senior leader communication, *65t*, 89–92
senior leader communication templates, *90t*, *91t*, 92
social media strategy, *74t*
societal responsibilities, *66t*, 110
SPA (single point accountable), 35–36
"speed of service" measurement, 132
stakeholder management, 35
state award programs, 8–10, 15–16, 29–30, 31
strategic measurement guidance
  80/20 rule, 134–135
  appropriate comparisons, 128, 140–141
  COMPARE, 141
  external comparisons, 136–139
  feedback, 135–136
  MEASURE, 133–134
  scorecard development process, 131–133
strategic planning guidance
  desired outcomes, 130–131
  key stakeholder groups, 131
  objectives, *68t*, *121–122t*, 127–132
  top decile default, 127–130
strategic planning process, *67t*, 115–117

strategic plan summary, *116t*
strategy, key approach
recommendations, *67–71t*
succession planning, *82t*
supply chain management, *86t*
supply chain measures, 110
SWOT analysis, *120–121f*

T

"The Management Century"
(Kiechel), 1
timetables, *125t*
top decile performance, 127–130
trends and comparisons, 142–143

U

"upstream" indicators, 132

V

voice of the customer (VOC) process,
71t

W–Z

who/what/when template, *146t*
workforce
benefits management, *81t*
change management, *79t*
engagement management, *81t*
key approach recommendations,
79–82t
performance management, *81t*
planning process, *70t*, *79t*
recruitment and retention, *80t*
workplace HSSA program, *80t*
work system evaluation processes, *67t*